A LAYMAN IN THE DESERT

Monastic Wisdom for a Life in the World

A Layman in the Desert

Monastic Wisdom for a Life in the World

Daniel G. Opperwall

ST VLADIMIR'S SEMINARY PRESS
YONKERS, NEW YORK
2015

Library of Congress Cataloging-in-Publication Data

Opperwall, Daniel G.
  A layman in the desert : monastic wisdom for a life in the world / Daniel
G. Opperwall
      pages cm
  ISBN 978-0-88141-522-3 (pbk.)—ISBN 978-0-88141-523-0 (electronic)
  1.   Spiritual life—Orthodox Eastern Church. 2.   Christian life—
Orthodox Eastern authors. 3.   Cassian, John, approximately 360–
approximately 435. Collationes patrum XXIV. 4.   Monastic and religious
life—Early works to 1800. 5.   Asceticism—Early works to 1800.
  I.   Title.
  BX382.O67 2015
  248.4'819—DC23
                                                                    2015019885

ST VLADIMIR'S SEMINARY PRESS
575 Scarsdale Road, Yonkers, NY 10707
www.svspress.com • 1-800-204-2665

ISBN 978-0-88141-522-3

Table of Contents

Acknowledgments

Many people read drafts of the manuscript, and their comments have been invaluable. Erica Roebbelen, Bethany Reid, Jennifer Haas, John Jobe, and all the people of All Saints of North America Orthodox Church provided much insight. I owe a special thanks to my beloved cousin and goddaughter, Mary-Helen Galluchi-Wright, whose scholarly and editorial input helped greatly to strengthen my early drafts. I owe thanks also to Joel Haas, Greg Wiebe, Sara Hillis, and especially Micah Erwin and Sean Reid, whose thoughts and wranglings provided the inspiration for this book; as St Germanus with St John, so we have walked through life's deserts and I pray that our wanderings are far from over. My thanks go also to Dr Augustine Casiday for his indispensable comments and sharp scholarly eye.

To my spiritual father, Dom James of Christminster, I owe an eternal debt, both for comments on the manuscript, and for the spiritual guidance needed to write it in the first place. My greatest thanks goes to my family. To my children, Patricia and Theodore, for their patience and love, and to my wife Eleni, for her comments on the book, and especially for teaching me to love and be loved better every day; her beautiful soul has inspired most of my own favorite passages, and her constant forgiveness and support has provided the space for them to be written.

I dedicate this book to my godchildren, Olivia, David, Joel, Jennifer, Michael, Dmitri, Justina, Mary Helen, and Bruno. May it be of some service in your lives when I, inevitably, fail to be.

Preface

A few years ago I was challenged by a critique of Orthodox Christianity leveled by a close friend who was in the process of leaving the Church. "When you face facts," he said, "you realize that if you really want to live the Orthodox life in its fullness, you have to become a monk." As much as I wished to offer a counter-point, I found myself unable. In fact, I even grudgingly agreed with his view. After all, there we stood, two converts living in the world, struggling to understand the Orthodox faith, and seemingly ever surrounded in that pursuit by monastic religiosity, monastic thought, and, above all, monastic literature. The last of these was perhaps the biggest source of our consternation. We could see quite well that nearly all the great spiritual writings of the Church, both ancient and modern, were composed by monks and nuns, or at the very least by priests and deacons. Such spiritual classics enticed our hearts with thoughts of scaling the summit of holiness by way of a life lived in the desert or monastery. For my friend, the realization that such a life was now wholly impossible for him (he was married with a new baby) became a profound burden that contributed to his walking away from the Church entirely.

I had raised a very similar objection myself once. I was on Mt Athos speaking with a priest-monk about the Christian life. I had recently gotten engaged, and I presented to the monk the same dilemma that my brother in Christ would later present to me. Was I not taking on a second-rate Orthodox lifestyle by getting married and embracing a life in the world? This monk of the Holy Mountain brushed the idea aside. "What is a monastery?" he asked me, and provided an answer, "A monastery is merely a place where people come to help one another to salvation. Your home as a married man should be no different from that." They were comforting words, and expressed a notion I had encountered many times before. Everywhere one turns in the Church, one is assured that, indeed, Orthodox life in the world can lead to salvation just as much as monastic life can.

As far as I can tell, there is no real debate in the Church about this idea, at least not at a fundamental level. The life of a non-monastic is as much a Christian life as any other, of this we are assured. And yet, one can often feel—as my friend and I did—that the Church merely pays lip-service to this teaching. We in the world can get the sense that we are being patted on the head by the monks, nuns and pastors around us. "Sure, your little life is just as good as ours!" we hear them saying, yet then we observe and, perhaps more importantly, read about lives wherein prayer and liturgy, fasting and sacrament, are the center of everything, and we wonder how our lives of work and family, money and property can possibly be "just as good." Immersed in the sayings of the Desert Fathers, the *Ladder of Divine Ascent,* the *Philokalia* and many more, we are often heartened, and grow in wisdom—yet our sense that life in the world is second-rate tends to grow along with our understanding of Christian spirituality. What ought we to make of this problem?

I have come to think that the key issue facing those lay people who, like me and my friend, find monastic literature as discouraging as it is helpful, is that we have paid too little attention in the English-speaking Church to the problem of translating this literature *conceptually.* We have the good fortune of an ever-increasing number of linguistic translations into English of great spiritual writings from across the many centuries and nations touched by the Orthodox Church, but we have not sufficiently attended to the theoretical problem of how these kinds of writings—especially when written by monks and nuns—can be made valuable for people living in a profoundly different context. How, we might ask, can a married person learn about chastity from ancient celibates? How can a wealthy person in the world learn about charity from people who owned nothing? How can a construction worker learn about fasting from people who ate little more than a biscuit every day?

It often seems that we Orthodox only end up spinning our wheels when we try to answer questions like these with reference to monastic literature. While we probably have a clear sense that there *is* something to be learned about such topics there, we do not always have a good picture of how to really find this value while also respecting the basic integrity and purpose of these texts.

One of the key sources of this problem is that we have not developed a sufficiently clear sense of what Orthodox life in the world is really about at a theoretical level, rather than a practical one. In today's Church, we are more and more surrounded by resources, from good pastors, to good books, that provide a great deal of guidance on the practicalities of worldly life. We are, for instance, encouraged to confess more often, commune more often, and go to church more often. Perhaps we are advised to repeat the Jesus Prayer on the bus, eat a little later during lent, or light a candle in church for a colleague who has done wrong by us—excellent practices and easily carried out. Yet, we seldom seem to reflect on what life as a lay person really is at its core—what its essential spiritual character and purpose are—and as a result we tend to misunderstand ourselves, our place in the Church, and our path to salvation. When we pick up books by monks and nuns without a strong understanding of who *we* are, we face a tremendous barrier to understanding their meaning as it relates to our own lives.

This is in part because we often seem to think of Christians in the world as sub-novice monks or nuns living an extremely pared-down form of monastic life. We see ourselves doing this by catching moments of peace, silence and prayer when we can, fasting as we are able, receiving the Eucharist at most once a week, and confessing to a spiritual father (if we are fortunate to have one) or our parish priest every month or so. We often seem to think to ourselves, "do what the monks and nuns do as much as you can, though you will not be able to do very much of it. Find moments to do it more, and live for these moments, braving the rough waters between." There is, of course, a serious problem with this approach. In the main, it encourages us to profoundly compartmentalize ourselves and our lives. It becomes very hard for us to see ourselves as Christians in any meaningful way during those times when we are at the office and actually working, or at home cooking dinner for the family, or downtown doing our shopping. We begin to see these activities as accidentals—unavoidable for us, of course, but merely necessary impediments to the real work of our spiritual lives, which we are trying to live as those "sub-novice" monks and nuns in the city. For some, the result is despair and frustration; in trying to live a monk's life in the world, we fail and curse ourselves for weakness. For others, and indeed probably most, thinking like a "sub-novice" ends in attempts to make life ever "easier" on ourselves spiritually. We may fast less rigorously, pray less often, or attend to other business on Sunday mornings. Hopeless as it is to become a true monk or nun while raising a family, we merely let ourselves go completely. Indeed, a startling number of Orthodox Christians today have slipped into such patterns over the course of generations to the point that nearly the whole of their Christian life often amounts to the lighting of a candle on Pascha night before departing prior to the liturgy in order to get to bed on time. Such people have become the ultimate "sub-novice" monks, first dividing worldly concerns from spiritual ones in their minds, and then allowing these worldly concerns to take more and more of their time until they have stripped away everything of spirituality down to the very last and most sacred remnants, and these often preserved only thanks to mysterious pangs of conscience.

When not casting ourselves as "sub-novice" monastics, we Orthodox lay people, especially those who are devout, are often tempted to begin thinking of ourselves as "sub-sub-deacons" whose salvation is to be found primarily in and through our local parish church. Part of the reason for this may be the fact that many, perhaps most, of the books being written today specifically for Orthodox Christian lay people in the world are being written by priests, and thus bear much of a priest's perspective. A parish priest, it is true, lives a great deal of his life under the same circumstances as a lay person. Yet, a parish priest has the burden and luxury of building his life in Christ on his ministry. For the priest, salvation is found especially in and through the parish and his attentive work as a pastor and liturgist. For the lay person, however, the parish cannot really be the primary place in which salvation is sought because it is not the primary place in which lay people live their lives. Indeed, even the most devoted and active of parish members (and we should be devoted and active) almost certainly spends less time on parish life than in cooking daily meals, to say nothing about going to work and tending to the family. We are no more "sub-sub-deacons" than we are "sub-novices."

When we see life in the world as amounting to a series of responsibilities that get in the way of real Christian life, then a spiritual break-down becomes virtually inevitable. If we think we are being saved only in those times that we can get away from work, family, society and the like, then we will find our faith is slowly extinguished by the demands of those things upon us, or marked by continuous despair, or even worse (and even more common)—both. Indeed, many are the Orthodox Christians today who continually neglect the spiritual "side" of their lives, and, when pressed, feel real regret and shame in face of this neglect, while nonetheless thinking themselves powerless to reverse it. To be assaulted all at once by spiritual malaise, guilt, and despair is an agonizing state of affairs indeed.

In the same way, when tacitly operating on the assumption that we are something like "sub-novices," we tend to find ourselves frustrated as we read the Church's great monastic literature. This should come as no surprise. Such literature calls us to so much more rigor than we think ourselves capable of cultivating that we can be forced to conclude one of two things. Either we are awfully lazy as Christians given how little we are able to model our lives after the spiritual masters, or those masters were different from us as people in some fundamental way—like angelic beings as compared to mere mortals. In the first case we grow despairing, in the second we toss monastic literature aside and fail to learn from its wisdom.

As such, if we are to make any use at all of the great spiritual classics, we must first shake off the temptation to see ourselves as "sub-novices" while reading it. We must, instead, recognize that for lay life to be a life in which we struggle seriously for our salvation, it must be understood as a life profoundly and genuinely lived *in the world*. Rather than seeing the work of salvation as what happens in those moments stolen away from our worldly cares and devoted to worship and prayer, we must see the work of our salvation as taking place mainly *through* our daily lives—*through* the things we spend most of our time doing. We must seek not merely to pray more, and, for instance, work in the evening less—but rather to find ways to be seeking our salvation *by way of* things like work, or chores, or raising our children. This is not to say that we should abandon things like prayer—far from it. It is, rather, to note that if we assume that those things on which we spend the vast majority of our time contribute nothing to our salvation, then our lives will, indeed, be mostly occupied by wide spiritual waste-lands, and no amount of wisdom from the monastic classics will be capable of helping us to turn such lives into green pastures.

In order to make monastic literature useful to us, then, we must first recognize that modern lay people and the monastic authors who have written most of the Church's spiritual classics struggle for salvation in fundamentally different *arenas* with different rules and different requirements. They are not combatants in the same location, some of whom have a lot more time for the battle than others. Instead, each finds herself in a separate place of contest. Each arena provides the Christian with tremendous opportunities for growth in Christ, and each is riven with its own brand of temptations and opportunities to fall further from God. If we are to read works by people struggling in one arena, then to go out and apply them in another, we must, quite obviously, think a lot about what is the same and what is different between these two spaces.

We do not do enough of this in the English-speaking Church today.

There is a second key mistake that we often make in our assumptions about the essential nature of life in the world, which mistake makes monastic literature difficult to approach. We often conceive of worldly life as merely a kind of default existence that anyone who is not specially called to monasticism or ordination simply ends up leading. We assume that it is only the monk, nun or priest who has a *special* call, while the married woman, for instance, has merely been passed by. It is easy to see why this feels natural to most of us. We all grow up as lay people. None of our parents are monks and nuns, and those few who grow up in the families of clergy are not, in youth at least, clergy themselves. We begin as lay people, and so we see this as our natural existence, disrupted for only a few select individuals who become monastics or priests, and continued for the rest of us. But, as natural as it is to think of lay life in this way, we must not allow ourselves to approach it merely in these terms. Instead, every one of us should, indeed must, treat lay life as a calling just the way we think of monasticism and ordination. We must sit down with ourselves and with God in prayer to discern if life in the world really is what we are meant for, and if we discover that it is, we must treat this call with the same seriousness with which we would treat a call to a hermit's life in the desert. We are not lay people simply because we happen not to be monks or priests. We are lay people because God wills that we lead a life seeking our salvation through the world. If we do not accept lay life as a holy calling, then we will gain nothing by reading the writings of people who believed that every single moment of their lives was meant to be devoted to God.

Reading monastic literature without a sense that lay life is a holy calling, and without recognizing that it is a calling that involves seeking salvation *through* struggle in the arena of life in the world, makes this literature very hard for us to comprehend and apply. So, why do we bother to read it at all? Perhaps it is better merely to leave it aside in order to avoid confusion and possible despair.

I have, in fact, encountered people in the Church who recommend this approach explicitly. Yet, I myself have never been quite comfortable with it. Throughout the history of the Church, people in the world have been guided by the lives and wisdom of monks and nuns whose prayers, words, and especially writings have brought countless souls closer to God. This bears witness to an important fact. While the life of a lay person is a special calling in which salvation is sought in a fundamentally different *arena* from that of the monk, nun, or the priest, it is *not* one in which salvation is sought through fundamentally different *means*. Our spiritual armor, while worn in two different battles, is made of the same metal—indeed, we have put on the same Christ in our baptism. Salvation itself is one and the same for all Christians, regardless of where they strive for it. Gabriel Bunge expresses this well.

> Lay people and monks do not each have their own "spirituality," and the Holy Spirit, whom they all receive at baptism, is one. The enemies and adversaries of the Christian are the same at all times no matter how well they disguise themselves. Victory will be gained also in one and the same manner, even when at first sight lay people and monks do not always put the same means into action.[1]

For this reason, all Orthodox Christians can and should seek the wisdom of monks and nuns, including through their writings, because it is they who reflect most deeply and most often on the *means* for gaining the victory we seek. While they may, understandably, not write very much about the arena in which we lay people struggle, their insight into the nature of the Christian armor used in that struggle is absolutely indispensable for all of us.

To read monastic literature well, then, we need to attend to the task of discussing how to really use this armor in our own arena. We cannot rely on people living in the desert or monastery to do this work for us—at least not in their writings for other monks and

---

[1]   Gabriel Bunge, *Despondency: The Spiritual Teaching of Evagrius Pontus* (Crestwood: St Vladimir's Seminary, 2012), 33.

nuns. While monastics past and present are anything but a pack of naive innocents who know nothing of the world, their purposeful and God-ordained retreat from that world (though it exists only to a degree, of course) really does present a barrier for those of us who wish to learn about the Christian life from them. As the desert mother battles the great lion of human solitude in the wilderness, and writes about this battle for other nuns, the modern lay woman fends off the spiritual bears hiding in her constant interactions with co-workers, family members, or people in the news. As the renowned elder struggles down the tigers of boredom and malaise in his cell, the layman fends off the gladiators of having all too much to distract him, and all too much to do. We must translate the wisdom of those who best understood the unified armor of Christian faith such as to apply it to the battle that takes place in the arena in which we in the world have been called to contend.

In this book I give my response to the despair of my old friend in light of all these considerations. I offer an essay toward the broad project of conceptually translating Orthodox monastic literature from the context in which it was written to the lives of modern lay people. I present such a conceptual translation of one small portion of the vast canon of Orthodox monastic literature. Of the many available collections written over the two thousand years of Church history, I have chosen to work with St John Cassian's *Conferences.* There are several reasons for this.

First, the text of the *Conferences* constitutes a fairly compact collection by a single author, and is thus much easier to assess as a whole than, for example, the sprawling (albeit beautifully so) *Philokalia.* Second, the complete text of the *Conferences* is readily available in English.[2] Third, the *Conferences* are worth the attention.

---

[2]   Best is the translation of Boniface Ramsey, *John Cassian: The Conferences* (New York: Newman, 1997). Orthodox readers should be aware that some of Ramsey's notes and commentary (especially to *Conference* 13) reflect a specifically Roman Catholic viewpoint. The much older translation of Edward Gibson, "The Works of John Cassian" in *A Select Library of the Nicene and Post Nicene Fathers of the Christian Church* Second Series, Vol XI, ed Philip Schaff and Henry Wace (Grand Rapids:

They are among the most influential works of Orthodox spiritual literature, and they deal with the foundational era of the Christian monastic movement. They were written in the early fifth century in Latin by St John Cassian. St John was also a Greek speaker (though Latin was probably his native tongue), and thus was fluent in the two great languages of the Roman Empire, giving him access to the fullness of its intellectual and spiritual tradition. St John was extremely well traveled, had myriad connections in ecclesiastical circles across the empire, and has maintained the highest reputation as a spiritual teacher from his own time to the present day.[3] Thus, in the *Conferences*, we read as a deeply influential saint records some of the teachings of the first and second generations of Orthodox desert monks whose ideas about monastic life became foundational to the Tradition East and West.

The fourth reason for choosing the *Conferences* is that they are organized around the teachings of particular desert fathers on specific topics regarding the Christian life of hermits. This makes it especially easy to identify the most important concepts underlying the teachings of these fathers, and thus to subsequently raise questions about how to apply these teachings in the world—which is to say, to translate them as we have set out to do. Fifth, and most importantly, the *Conferences* record extended conversations between St John, his companion St Germanus, and the many desert fathers with whom they spoke while traveling in Egypt. Although it is impossible that St John has recorded his conversations with these fathers verbatim, they are nonetheless based on real encounters

Eerdmans) is seldom ideal for a modern reader, but it has the advantage of being available for free online.

[3]   St John was born fairly well-off, perhaps near Romania, lived in Palestine as a monk for some time, visited the Egyptian desert and the first great generation of hermits there at least twice and for as much as a decade, was ordained deacon by St John Chrysostom in Constantinople, priest by Pope St Innocent in Rome, and ultimately founded two major monasteries near Marseilles, France. Quite the résumé! For a more detailed discussion of his life see Chapter One of Columba Stewart, *Cassian the Monk* (Oxford: Oxford, 1998). St John's feast day in the Orthodox Church is February 29.

between real people. As a result, they record questions and challenges leveled (usually by St Germanus) at the desert fathers, as well as those fathers' responses, in a way that gives them an openness and honesty that more heavily edited collections cannot rival. In sum, the *Conferences*, more than almost any other ancient text, let us sit at the feet of these great fathers and therefore allow us to be, for a little while, what the title of this book asks us to become: lay people in the desert.

Three last comments are important before we begin. First, I feel it incumbent to make it absolutely clear (if it is not already) that nothing written here is meant as a critique of monastic life in the Orthodox Church, either as it has existed in the past or exists in the present. If there are such critiques to be made, I am not qualified to present them. May God bless and keep our monasteries and hermits, and may the ranks of monks and nuns swell until our Lord and Savior's return!

Second, it is essential to make clear that this book is *not* meant for those who may themselves be discerning a call to monastic life. It is my hope that this book will make more real and accessible the Church's certain teaching that salvation is possible for lay people living in the world. Yet, I feel some concern that such a message may only make more complicated the difficult task facing those who feel they may be called by God to life as a monk or nun. To any who are not already committed lay people (or monastics), I offer a humble request to set this book aside until the path has become clear.

Finally, I feel it is important to warn the reader in advance that some sections of the *Conferences* and other similar monastic literature can be fairly troublesome and even spiritually dangerous, at least at first, to the lay reader. While the vast majority of what St John writes can be read by the laity without hesitation, portions of his works require caution if they are to be navigated without being misunderstood. Among the clearest examples of such a section in the *Conferences* is the story of Abba Theonas from

Conf. 21.I–X. Here, the young Theonas, feeling called to a monastic life, ultimately divorces his wife after she refuses to consent to living as a nun herself while remaining nominally married. The story is troubling in many ways, even to St John Cassian, as we will see in another chapter.[4] For the moment, though, we should simply note that when reading about monks like Abba Theonas we may worry too much that our small efforts toward virtue are so minuscule as to be without meaning, or might think we are meant to take an example like his literally. The end result of such thoughts, if we are not on our guard, can be despair and an impulse to give up on the Christian life. Indeed, the enemy can strike even as we read the stories of some of the holiest people in history. The reader should be aware, and, if he or she should begin to experience such despair when reading the *Conferences* or any other monastic work, set them aside for a time. A conversation with a parish priest may offer some comfort and a reminder that life in the world can be a life of holiness. I also pray that this book will be of some help to those in such a situation. Above all, Orthodox Christians should rest assured in one conclusion: when read and understood correctly, nothing in St John's writings, or any other Orthodox monastic work, ought to leave us despairing of our salvation, God's love, or even our own capacity as people in the world to realize virtue and holiness through his grace.

[4]   See p. 123*ff.*

CHAPTER I

The Purpose and Method of Christian Life

But now having been set free from sin, and having become slaves of God, you have your fruit to holiness, and the end, everlasting life.
Romans 6.22[1]

The Goal and *Telos* of Christian Life

In the preface we noted that Christian salvation is fundamentally the same, whether pursued in the world or through monasticism. It is this foundational unity, which is the unity of the Holy Spirit himself, that makes monastic spirituality and literature so valuable for the lay Orthodox. Lay and monastic life have the same purpose. In order to begin the work of applying the key teachings of the *Conferences* to life in the world, then, we need to discuss what this basic purpose of a Christian's life is according to the fathers of the desert.

Conveniently for us, the purpose of Christian life is precisely the topic with which St John opens the *Conferences*, recording the teachings of Abba Moses on the point.[2] According to Abba Moses,

---

[1] Scriptural quotations, other than those appearing directly in passages from the *Conferences*, are quoted from, for the New Testament, from the New King James Version ®. Copyright © 1982 by Thomas Nelson, Inc. and, for the Old Testament, the St Athanasius Academy Septuagint TM. Copyright © 2008 by St Athanasius Academy of Orthodox Theology. Used by permission. All rights reserved. These are the texts that appear in the *Orthodox Study Bible.*

[2] Throughout our discussion of the *Conferences* we will attribute particular passages, and the ideas contained within them, to the specific fathers (abbas) to whom St John Cassian attributes them. We do so in order to make certain ideas more easy to reference, and to reflect the basic design of St John's text. We do

a monk's life has a "goal," (also referred to by him with the Greek word *scopos*, meaning "target") and this life has a proper "end" or *telos* (simply the Greek word for "end").[3] These terms require some definition, and Abba Moses gives it. He explains that every human pursuit, whether spiritual or worldly, has both a *telos* and a goal. The two go together, but are distinct. One example he gives is a farmer, whose sought-after *telos* is a comfortable life with enough to eat, but who pursues the specific goal of getting his fields weeded and cleared of stones in order to eventually attain this *telos*.[4] The farmer's goal, as any goal in Abba Moses' particular usage here, is an intermediary to his *telos*. What is more, and this is important, the farmer's goal is something he hopes to accomplish by a specific action, or set of actions, while his *telos* is a state of being that he wishes to attain. His goal, then, is something he works toward concretely, while his *telos* is a state that he seeks only through the goal. A second example used by Abba Moses illustrates well this point about the difference between the two. A person, he says, who desires fame and glory might pursue a particular political office of high esteem.[5] Such a person works concretely toward the goal of becoming, say, a governor, while his desired *telos* is to *be* famous and powerful, something he cannot strive for directly, but will arise for him if and when he accomplishes his goal.

A *telos*, then, is the reason for pursuing a particular goal. What is more, the two are tied together in that a *telos* follows on the attainment of a goal by necessity. If one attains her goal, she will

not do so out of ignorance that in the *Conferences* St John is "presenting his own theological synthesis as their teaching," as is noted correctly in Stewart, *Cassian the Monk*, p. 28 and other scholars.

[3]   In most cases below, we will employ the term *telos* rather than its translation, "end," simply in order to avoid the possible confusion that can arise from such phrases as "the end of Christian life," which could appear to indicate death. *Telos* will be clear in every context. Readers consulting the Latin text will note that the term usually employed by Abba Moses as a translation of *telos* is *finis*. See *Conf.* I.II.I.

[4]   *Conf.* I.IV.2.

[5]   *Conf.* I.IV.2.

necessarily reach her *telos*, and, conversely, if one fails to attain her goal, she cannot reach the desired *telos*. Abba Moses uses yet another illustration here, this time describing how people who wish to win an archery contest aim at a small target (their goal) and when they hit it, they immediately receive a prize (their *telos*). However, if an archer loses sight of his target, he will by definition be unable to obtain his prize.[6] Goal and *telos* are thus conceptually distinct, but they go necessarily together.

With clear definitions of what a goal and *telos* are as concepts, Abba Moses now describes the goal and *telos* of Christian monks specifically.

> The *telos* of our [monastic] commitment, as we noted, is the kingdom of God or the kingdom of heaven; but the immediate goal (*scopos*) is purity of heart, without which it is impossible for anyone to get to the *telos* that we are talking about. Fixing our eyes steadily on this goal, then … let us make for it without wavering.[7]

Abba Moses goes on to say that the work of the monk is aimed concretely at attaining purity of heart, and if he attains this goal, the natural result, its *telos*, will be the kingdom of God. We will explain what he means by these latter terms ("purity of heart" and "kingdom of God") in just a moment.

We must first make note, however, that it will be an operating principle for us that the lay Christian has the same goal and *telos* as the monk. Our use of this principle needs only a little justification. One must merely think about what it would mean to argue that a lay person and a monk actually differ in their *telos* or goal to see why it makes plain sense to assume that they do not. Could one reasonably argue that a lay Christian is not called to pursue purity of heart, or to attain the kingdom of God? Even without fully defining these terms yet, it is clear that one could not. For all people,

---

[6] *Conf.* I.V.I.
[7] *Conf.* I.IV.3. Translations of the *Conferences* are my own unless noted as adaptations of Gibson's translation, previously referenced. I have used the Latin texts from the *Sources Chrétiennes* series.

then, the goal of Christian life is purity of heart, while its *telos* is the kingdom of God.

So, what do the terms "purity of heart" and "kingdom of God" mean? We begin with purity of heart. Abba Moses speaks at quite some length about what it is, as well as what it is not. First, we will look at what Abba Moses says about purity of heart in positive terms—what he says about what it actively is.

Abba Moses connects purity of heart to a variety of other terms and concepts that help give us a picture of what it means to him. At one point, for example, he defines it simply as "holiness," a term he does not further discuss, but one that is probably quite familiar to most readers.[8] Elsewhere he connects purity of heart to tranquility.[9] By "tranquility," Abba Moses probably means the ability to rein in the mind, avoiding the problem of having one's thoughts run off in all directions uncontrolled.[10] As an extension of this, tranquility, for him, also appears to involve the ability to direct oneself away from evil and sinful thoughts toward holy and pure ones.[11] Abba Moses finally connects purity of heart explicitly with love, saying that purity of heart is specifically the kind of love that St Paul talks about when he says that "if I gave all my goods to feed the poor...but I did not have love, it would profit me nothing."[12]

Holiness, tranquility, love—these things define purity of heart for Abba Moses, and from these three terms alone, we get a good picture of what it means. Still, this is not all that Abba Moses has to say about purity of heart. Indeed, he is in fact probably most clear about what it really is when talking about what it is *not*.

> And from this it clearly follows that perfection is not arrived at simply by self-denial, and the giving up of all our goods...unless there is that love, the details of which the apostle describes

---

[8]   *Conf.* I.V.2.
[9]   *Conf.* I.VII.4.
[10] *Conf.* I.V.4.
[11] *Conf.* I.XVII.1–2.
[12] I Cor 13:3. quoted in *Conf.* I.VI.3.

[I Cor 13.3], which consists in purity of heart alone. For "not to be envious," "not to be puffed up, not to be angry, not to do any wrong, not to seek one's own, not to rejoice in iniquity, not to think evil" etc., what is all this except ever to offer to God a perfect and clean heart, and to keep it free from all passions?[13]

Purity of heart, for Abba Moses, is the state of the soul in absence of the passions. By passions he means, as the passage implies, any of the myriad human temptations and inclinations to evil, along with the active carrying out of such inclinations. He lists some of the worst such passions here directly, saying that in *not* engaging these passions, the human being offers God a pure heart. Purity of heart, then, is what is left in us when sin has been dismissed, when all the accouterments of vice are set aside, and, in short, when the human being ceases to fall away from holiness, tranquility and love. To reach this state is the goal of all Christians according to Abba Moses. We will return to the question of how Christians ought to work toward this goal, and say a little more about what purity of heart looks like in practice, when we discuss the virtues in the next section of this chapter.

First, though, we need to define the Christian *telos*, which is to say, the kingdom of God, a little more clearly.[14] As with purity of heart, Abba Moses says a great deal about it over the course of his conference. The first thing with which he connects the kingdom of God is eternal life.

So then, the *telos* of our [monastic] commitment is, to quote the apostle, eternal life—for he says "having, indeed, your fruit unto holiness and your *telos*, eternal life" [Rom 6.22]. Our immediate goal, though, is purity of heart, which he rightly dubs "holiness" here. Without this, our noted *telos* cannot be gained. Indeed, the apostle could have even substituted these very terms and said

---

13   *Conf.* I.VI.3. Translation adapted from Gibson.
14   Note that Abba Moses sometimes uses the phrase "kingdom of heaven" with the same meaning as "kingdom of God" as we have already seen him do in a quotation on p. 23.

"having, indeed, your 'immediate goal' in 'purity of heart' and your *telos* eternal life."[15]

Having already stated that the *telos* of Christian life is the kingdom of God, Abba Moses here also claims that this *telos* is eternal life, thus directly equating the two on the grounds of Paul's words in Romans. For this reason, Abba Moses sees the kingdom of God and death, which he considers to be connected to the kingdom of the devil, to be contrasting concepts.

> Where the kingdom of God is, doubtless, there abides eternal life. And where the kingdom of the devil is, no doubt, there is death and hades. There a person can never praise the Lord, in accordance with the understanding of the prophet who says "the dead do not praise you, Lord—no, not any who descend into hades" [Psalm 113:17] (here, without a doubt, he means sin).[16]

Where there is death, there is hell, and hell, according to this passage, is in some sense sin itself. For Abba Moses, the kingdom of God is precisely where the death of sin is not, and thus by extension it is where unending life resides. Beyond the connection to eternal life and contrast to death and sin, this passage also links the kingdom of God to the praise of God. It does so by noting the inability to offer this praise for those who exist in death and sin. The kingdom, then, is in some sense an unending life of God's praise, divorced from death, hell, and all that they represent.

Elsewhere, Abba Moses connects the kingdom of God with knowledge of truth, righteousness, peace, and above all, joy.

> But nothing else can be "within you," but knowledge or ignorance of truth, and delight either in vice or in virtue, through which we prepare a kingdom for the devil or for Christ in our heart. The apostle describes the character of this kingdom when he says, "for the kingdom of God is not food and drink, but righteousness and peace and joy in the Holy Spirit" [Rom 14.7]. And so, if the kingdom of God is within us, and righteousness and peace

---

[15]   *Conf.* I.V.2.
[16]   *Conf.* I.XIV.2.

and joy are indeed that very kingdom itself ... what should we imagine it to be except perpetual and lasting joy?[17]

The *telos* of the Christian is righteousness, peace and joy, and these things, in accordance with the teachings of Paul, are the kingdom of God residing within the human being. To know the truth and to love these things is to dwell in the kingdom, says Abba Moses.

In this vein, the difference between the kingdom of God and God himself can begin to blur in the words of the Abba. For example, he notes that the reason Christians pursue their goal, purity of heart, is to attain the *telos* of a permanent connection not just to holy things, ideas or states associated with God, but to God himself.

> This, then, must be our primary undertaking—this the never-altered destination and never-failing pursuit of the heart—that the mind might always cling to things divine and to God.[18]

Much may be implied in this small comment. If, as according to this passage, attaining purity of heart brings a state in which one is totally attached to God, then this *telos* is, in fact, God himself in some sense. Another passage bears this out a little more. Here, Abba Moses quotes Isaiah at length to illustrate the state of the soul in the kingdom of God, evoking, as he does, the experience of the light that is God himself.

> I will establish your rulers in peace and your bishops in righteousness. Unrighteousness shall no longer be heard in your land, neither destruction nor distress within your boundaries, but your walls shall be called Salvation, and your gates Sculptured Work. The sun shall no longer be your light by day, nor shall the rising of the moon shine on you at night, but the Lord shall be your everlasting light, and God, your glory. For your sun shall no longer set, nor shall your moon be eclipsed, for the Lord shall be your everlasting light, and the days of your mourning shall be fulfilled.[19]

---

[17] *Conf.* I.XIII.2–3. Translation adapted from Gibson.
[18] *Conf.* I.VIII.I.
[19] Is 60.17–20.

While neither the language of *theosis* (divinization), nor that of the uncreated light appear explicitly in the writings of St John Cassian, a nascent conception of *theosis* and divine light may well be in evidence in the two above-quoted passages. There is a sense here that the connection points between God and his kingdom are so close as to essentially identify the two. Ultimately, an Orthodox Christian may well conclude, the knowledge, righteousness, peace, joy, eternal life, and ever-present light that Abba Moses refers to in describing the kingdom are all in some sense God as present with and in his human creatures, a presence that transforms these creatures into God in his energies (to use some much later theological terminology for a moment). Indeed, in one of the most beautiful passages in all the *Conferences,* Abba Isaac describes this desired human *telos* in a way consistent with such a reading.

> For then that prayer of the Savior will be perfectly realized in us—that prayer that he prayed to the Father for his disciples, asking … "that they may be one, as you in me and I in you, that they may also be one in us" [Jn 17.21].... This will come to be when all our love, all our desire, all our effort, all our intention, all our thought—every moment we live through, what we say, what we breathe—when it all becomes God, and the unity that now exists for the Father with the Son and the Son with the Father is brought over into our awareness, so that as he loved us with an earnest and pure and unbreakable love, we also may cling to him by an eternal, inseparable bond of affection, so that, indeed, we are so fused with him that whatever we breathe, whatever we think, whatever we say, is God.[20]

We seek unity with God in a profound and transcendent way. This is the intended *telos* of all human beings, which the Christian consciously desires.

In accordance with his understanding of our goal and *telos,* Abba Moses now teaches that the Christian must constantly remain focused on working *not* essentially for the *telos* of the kingdom, but

---

20   *Conf.* 10.VII.1–2.

rather on working toward the goal of purity of heart, never losing sight of this goal.

> And so, when [purity of heart] is set before us, we shall always direct our actions and thoughts straight toward the attainment of it; for if it is not constantly before our eyes, it will not only make all our toils vain and useless, and force them to be endured to no purpose and without any reward, but it will also excite all kinds of chaotic thoughts in our minds.[21]

If the Christian forgets her goal, all is wasted, a lack of tranquility results, and life begins to fall apart for her. Thus, from Abba Moses' teaching we arrive at our summary observation about the purpose of Christian life according to the fathers of the *Conferences*. Christian life is meant to be a life in which absolutely every action, thought, and word is directed toward obtaining purity of heart. When this purity of heart is reached, the Christian *telos*, the kingdom of God, becomes manifest. When it is forgotten, attaining the kingdom is impossible.

So, how do we get started in our work toward the goal of purity of heart that leads to the *telos* of the kingdom? Abba Moses has a simple reply. "The kingdom of God is experienced in purity of heart and spiritual knowledge through the exercise of virtues."[22] To a discussion of Christian virtues we now turn.

Virtues

According to the *Conferences*, to cultivate purity of heart means to live a life of Christian virtue. For the fathers, speaking about virtues is like placing the white light of purity of heart through a mental prism. Virtues are like the colors that make up the light, combining indivisibly into a single whole, but capable of being discussed on their own.

Many of the fathers in the *Conferences* talk at length about virtues, their nature, and how to cultivate them. The *Conferences* lack

---

21 *Conf.* I.V.2. Translation adapted from Gibson.
22 *Conf.* I.XIV.1.

a systematic list of the virtues, and one gets the sense in reading St John's works that they are too great in number to ever compile them exhaustively. Moreover, the fathers of the *Conferences* will often talk about specific kinds of practices or spiritual skills using the term "virtue." They seem not to have been influenced by later approaches to virtue that focus only on specific internal qualities within a human being. As such, their approach to the concept of virtues is rather fluid, and in our discussion here, we will follow the *Conferences* in this regard.

Here we will identify five key virtues that are important to the fathers of the desert. We have chosen the five below for three reasons. First, they are some of the most foundational in the *Conferences*. Second, these five virtues, in particular, will be important to understand from the start so that we may refer to them easily in the remaining chapters. Third, each of these virtues is cultivated within an individual human being—they are personal virtues. Many other important virtues, in contrast, can only become manifest in interactions between two or more people, and so can be thought of as relational virtues. Such relational virtues will be easier to examine in later chapters. The five virtues that we will address here are: detachment, discernment, discretion, humility, and balance.

The first virtue on our list is detachment. In essence, the state of detachment is that in which the Christian ceases to be concerned by earthly or material things—or even necessities—and is instead mentally occupied only with godly things. This is not to say that the Christian neglects basic needs, but rather that her mental and spiritual focus is never primarily upon these needs or the things that feed them. Detachment is the state in which the Christian entirely conforms to Christ's injunction in the Gospel of Matthew.

> Do not store up for yourselves treasures on earth, where moth and rust consume and where thieves break in and steal; but store up for yourselves treasures in heaven, where neither moth nor rust

consumes and where thieves do not break in and steal. For where your treasure is, there your heart will be also.[23]

Attachment to worldly things is a great temptation for all people, even monks, according to Abba Moses. For, while desert monks have very few possessions, if they do not attain detachment, then what little they own can become just as great a spiritual burden as vast wealth.

> For hence it arises that in the case of some who have despised the greatest possessions of this world—and not only large sums of gold and silver, but also large properties—we have seen them afterwards disturbed and excited over a pencil, or pin, or pen, or knife. However, if they kept their gaze steady out of a pure heart, they would certainly never allow such a thing to happen for trifles.... For often, too, some guard their books so jealously that they will not allow them to be even slightly moved or touched by anyone else, and from this fact they meet with occasions of impatience and death deriving from the very things that were meant to help them acquire patience and love.[24]

The fathers of the *Conferences* are abundantly clear in teaching that worldly and physical things are absolutely not spiritually evil in themselves, a point that we will discuss in further detail in chapter four. The problem with worldly things comes if the Christian becomes attached to them, and thus loses sight of the importance of purity of heart, as Abba Moses teaches here.

Detachment is critical to attaining purity of heart for fairly obvious reasons. If one prefers worldly concerns to divine ones, whether these concerns center on material objects and possessions, or things like money, power, and sex, then one is by definition not seeking God. To build on Abba Moses' analogy of the archer, focusing on the things of the world while still hoping for purity of heart is like trying to hit a target while keeping one's eyes and mind fixed on a bystander with whom one is having a deep conversation.

---

[23] Mt 6.19–21.
[24] *Conf* I.VI.I. Translation adapted from Gibson.

If what we seek are things divine, then to concern ourselves with things of the world cannot but guide as away from them.

We will discuss the virtue of detachment in much more detail in chapter four. For now, it is sufficient to present a basic definition of the concept. We must, however, discuss the next two virtues on our list in a little more detail right away. These are discernment and discretion.

Both discernment and discretion involve the Christian's development of a correct relationship with various ideas and concepts. They are intellectual virtues in that to display them means to recognize certain truths and realities clearly, without being deceived. Abba Moses defines discernment in the first conference as the ability first to avoid any kind of incorrect doctrine or idea that might lead a monk astray.

> Whatever has found entrance into our hearts, and whatever doctrine has been received by us, should be most carefully examined to see whether it has been purified by the divine and heavenly fire of the Holy Spirit ... or whether it comes from the pride of a worldly philosophy and is only pious in superficial appearance.[25]

Abba Moses continues by saying that he has known many monks who have been led astray by ideas that seemed, at first, to be consistent with a pious Christian life. Chief among these kinds of ideas, it would appear, are theological heresies of various sorts, teachings that encourage monks to return to a life in the world, and various prideful teachings about how to live the Christian life. Abba Moses then gives just a few examples, focusing on those ideas that lead monks into spiritual arrogance, such as the idea of going to extreme lengths in fasting, or desiring to become priests for prideful reasons.[26] He also highlights the problem of false interpretations of scripture that are disguised under apparent piety and truth,[27] and his mention of heresies above implies that one can be similarly

---

[25]   *Conf.* I.XX.2. Translation adapted from Gibson.
[26]   *Conf.* I.XX.3–5.
[27]   *Conf.* I.XX.4.

misled by false theological teachings, though he does not give any specific examples of these. Yet, the particulars of the various errors into which Abba Moses has seen his brothers fall are not what is most critical for us in trying to understand his concern about the problem of false teachings. What is important is that, for Abba Moses, there are a lot of ideas about Christian life and theology that may seem good and holy, but are not. It is the task of the Christian to develop discernment such as to recognize the truth from deception.

But how does one do this in principle? One crucial element of Abba Moses' understanding of discernment sheds light on how it is cultivated. For Abba Moses, the monk runs the risk of various intellectual errors when he begins to trust the instincts of his own mind too readily. Bad ideas are those that seem good to the one hearing them, but that have not met with the approval of the fathers.

> All these things, though they are contrary to our salvation and monastic commitment, can deceive the unskilled and incautious because they are covered with a sort of veil of compassion and religiosity. They imitate the coins of the true king since they appear to be completely pious, but they are not from the real mint—that is, from the proven and orthodox fathers.... The devil deceives when he has the appearance of holiness, "but he hates the sound of the watchman" [Prov 11.15 LXX], i.e. the power of discretion that comes from the words and warnings of the fathers.[28]

Discernment, it seems from Abba Moses' description, involves a certain kind of distrust for one's own spiritual and theological instincts in light of the devil's ability to use a little bit of truth to perpetrate a lie. One turns, in light of this distrust, to the fathers of the Church and so, over time, begins to develop a fluency with their teachings, and their correct interpretations of scripture. Eventually one starts to recognize, through discernment, the difference between true and false teachings of whatever sort.

---

[28] *Conf.* I.XX.6–8.

The Christian, then, must be on guard against doctrines and scriptural interpretations that lead to ruin—she must develop discernment to see such ideas for what they are. But perhaps even more pressing, according to the *Conferences*, is the need to develop discretion. According to the fathers of the *Conferences*, discretion is an intellectual virtue much like discernment, except a Christian applies discretion when considering not which ideas, doctrines, and scriptural interpretations to embrace, but when considering herself and her inner state, and deciding which practices to carry out, which things to say, and what to do in a given situation. All of the second conference, again delivered by Abba Moses, is dedicated to a discussion of the virtue of discretion. He reports that the great founder of the Orthodox desert monastic tradition, St Anthony, taught that discretion is the greatest of all the virtues. According to Anthony, discretion is what is meant by Christ when he talks of the eye being the light of the body in Matthew 6.22–23. The speaker in the following quotation is St Anthony.

> For this is discretion, which is termed in the gospel the "eye," "and light of the body," according to the Savior's saying: "the light of your body is your eye. If the eye is single, the whole body will be full of light, but if his eye is evil, your whole body will be full of darkness" [Mt 6.22–23]. This is because [the eye—discretion] considers every thought and action of a person; it oversees—surveys—all that must be done.[29]

Discretion, according to St Anthony and Abba Moses, is thus the virtue marked by a Christian's capacity to scrutinize all that he thinks, feels, and does, and hold it up against the standards of the truth. If a person's discretion, like the eye of the body, is in working order, all things are illuminated for him. Indeed, it is for this reason that Abba Moses says that "the birth-giver of all the virtues—the guardian and director of them—is discretion."[30] After all, one cannot possibly practice virtue without first recognizing

---

[29] *Conf.* 2.II.5. Translation adapted from Gibson.
[30] *Conf.* 2.IV.4.

through discretion whether one is acting, speaking, or thinking out of virtue or vice in a particular instance.

Much like the virtue of discernment, in order to develop discretion a monk must establish a correct relationship with the best teachers around him. As in the case of discernment, the monk must have a healthy distrust for his own judgment, and live in accordance with the wisdom of the elders. Abba Moses tells a brief story of a monk who worked harder in asceticism than any other, but still fell into error.

> [This monk] had lived for fifty years in this desert, keeping an exceptionally severe form of abstinence, and loved the isolation of solitude with particular enthusiasm. By what method, then, was he deluded by the deceiver after so many labors? ... Was it not that, lacking the virtue of discretion, he preferred to be guided by his own judgment rather than to obey the counsels and conference of the brothers and the regulations of the elders?[31]

This particular monk, Abba Moses goes on to report, fell into error by becoming so overzealous for asceticism that he refused even to celebrate Pascha with the other monks in the desert, and finally came to the point of accepting Satan who appeared to him as an angel of light. He then literally threw himself into a well, an act of delusion that ultimately killed him.[32] His essential problem was in trusting himself too much, and placing his own judgments in such absurdly high esteem that he ceased seeking out the opinions of other elders on spiritual questions. Had he merely worked to develop a little discretion with the help of the counsel of others, he would never have been tricked by demonic appearances.

As we will see throughout the remainder of this book, it is critical that Christians develop discretion in the face of whatever might tempt us in life. Whether inclined to over-reach in the practice of religion, like the monk above, or to forsake such practice and embrace a life of pleasures, whether prone to anger or to

---

[31]   *Conf.* 2.V.1–2.
[32]   *Conf.* 2.V.2–3.

laxity, whether likely to fall into materialism or neglect of love, the Christian must exercise discretion by examining herself and what she does in light of the teachings of the spiritual masters of the Church. What is more, as we will continually see in every chapter to follow, exercising discretion is the only means by which the Christian can begin to utilize her spiritual shortcomings as actual tools in the pursuit of purity of heart. If we do not see our own moments of failure, understand their nature, and recognize the path back to purity of heart, then life in the world will be more or less hopeless for us. Much more on this later, however.

According to the fathers of the *Conferences*, the result of developing discretion and discernment is the manifestation of the fourth virtue on our list, namely, balance. This balance is described by Abba Moses as the "royal road," upon which a monk is not made proud by virtue nor drawn down so as to give in to vice.[33] Christian life, Abba Moses assumes, invites one both to laxity and to possible over-corrections in the pursuit of purity of heart. Seeings one's particular failings in a certain direction, the person is tempted to go too far in the other, and vice-versa. It is interesting to observe that, throughout the *Conferences,* many of the desert fathers are much more concerned about teaching the importance of balance in the face of monks who engage in *too much* religious rigor—such as the monk who threw himself in a well—than in working to correct those who are lazy. For those of us living in the world, this may seem a little bit backwards in that most of us tend to be tempted toward falling into vice rather than toward an excess of fervor. However, for those ancient men and women who chose a life in the desert over a life in the city, it was evidently the case that deluded attempts at extreme piety were a more frequent problem than temptations to malaise. Regardless, to manifest the virtue of balance means not to fall into either trap.

For Abba Daniel, the speaker in the fourth conference, it is precisely in order that the Christian can learn to live a life of balance

---

[33] *Conf.* 2.II.4.

that God has created what may appear, to the untrained eye, to be a conflict between the flesh and the spirit within human beings. Abba Daniel begins by observing that the impulses of flesh and spirit are often contrary to one another.

> The flesh delights in wantonness and lust, but the spirit does not even tolerate natural desire. The one wants to have plenty of sleep, and to be satiated with food; the other is nourished with vigils and fasting, so as to be unwilling even to take sleep and food as is necessary for life.[34]

According to Abba Daniel, the human being is naturally inclined to try and find ways to attain the lofty desires of the spirit without ever setting aside any of the desires of the flesh; we want to have our cake and eat it. Abba Daniel describes the resultant state of monks who continually seek spiritual goods while trying to gratify bodily ones as "lukewarmness" and notes that it is impossible by pursuing such a lukewarm path to attain real perfection.[35] It is precisely because the will tends to desire this lukewarm state that the spirit and the flesh are led into conflict with one another by God.

> For when we give in to this free will of ours and want to let ourselves go in the direction of slackness, at once the desires of the flesh start up, and injure us with their sinful passions, and do not let us continue in that state of purity in which we delight.... But, if inflamed with fervor of spirit, we want to root out the works of the flesh, and without any regard to human weakness try to raise ourselves to excessive efforts toward virtue, the frailty of the flesh comes in, and recalls us and restrains us from that excess of spirit.[36]

Thus, for Abba Daniel, a kind of moderation results from the apparent conflict between flesh and spirit, the balance of the "royal road."[37] This life of balance is marked for him by sufficient, but

---

[34] *Conf.* 4.XI.2–3. Translation adapted from Gibson.
[35] *Conf.* 4.XII.1–2.
[36] *Conf.* 4.XII.2–3. Translation adapted from Gibson.
[37] *Conf.* 4.XII.5.

never excessive, attention paid to the needs of the flesh, and by continuous pursuit of the desires of the spirit. Balance is like the virtuous mirror-image of the vice of lukewarmness. Where the lukewarm monk fails properly to address the needs of his flesh (by overindulgence), and never really attends sufficiently to the needs of his spirit, the monk leading a life of balance gives both their due, and allows each to draw the other into its right place.

The understanding of what it means to be human that is implicit in teachings like those of Abba Daniel is important. For Abba Daniel, human beings are not spiritual creatures somehow trapped in a physical body (a teaching that was common to much of the non-Christian and gnostic philosophy of the day, and often perpetuated today), but instead are created by God to be physical *and* spiritual beings at the same time. To realize the virtue of balance, then, is to begin to realize the kind of existence for which every human being was created—a life of perfection both physical and spiritual. Imbalance, for the fathers of the desert, leads one to pay too much attention to one or the other aspect of the human person, and thus leads one not to be what God created all people to be.

Balance, we have already noted, can only be attained through discretion and discernment. Yet, there is another key virtue that the monk must seek if he is going to walk the royal road according to the *Conferences.* This is the fifth and final virtue on our list, namely, humility, which, according to Abba Moses, is the foundational virtue lying beneath a Christian's ability to practice discernment and discretion and thus, by extension, to live a life of balance. For Abba Moses, humility is first approached by the monk who sets aside his own will and judgment, and follows the advice of the elders. It is thus closely related to discretion and discernment as a prerequisite to both.

> True discretion, he said, is only acquired by true humility. The first sign of such humility comes when both everything one plans to do and everything one thinks are submitted to the elders for

examination, this done to the point that, thinking nothing of his own judgment, one yields to their guidance in everything.[38]

Abba Moses follows this statement with a story regarding one of the other monks in the desert who had taken to stealing a little bit of food every day, but who ultimately repented and confessed his actions to his elder. By bringing his sin out into the light through this act of humility, the young monk found himself freed from his guilt, his powers of discretion ultimately strengthened by the experience.[39]

Humility, like discernment and discretion, begins with a basic distrust of one's own judgments, and a submission of these judgments to one's spiritual elders. Yet, it means more than this in the *Conferences.* The Christian who seeks humility must also become aware of the limited power of his own works, and realize that it is only through God's grace that he can overcome temptations, embrace virtues, and walk the royal road of balance. In the fifth conference, Abba Serapion makes clear that the monk who manages to conquer some of his vices must not take any credit for the victory himself, but must realize that the victory belongs to God.

> Thus, we are assured by actual experience—and taught by countless passages in scripture—that we cannot overcome these powerful enemies by our own strength, but only with the aid and support of God. To him we must credit the whole of our success each day. On this point the Lord (through Moses) declares: "Do not say in your heart when the Lord your God has destroyed them in your sight: 'for my righteousness has the Lord guided me to possess this land, while these nations are destroyed for their wickedness'" [Deut 9.4].[40]

Here, Abba Serapion responds to one of the key problems that the monk (or any Christian) faces as he or she struggles to attain purity of heart. Success in such a pursuit presents the Christian with a

---

[38]   *Conf.* 2.X.1.
[39]   *Conf.* 2.XI.1–6.
[40]   *Conf.* 5.XV.2.

paradox—it must be acknowledged for the victory that it is, and yet it cannot be allowed to lead to pride and self-congratulation—things that would pull the Christian down into a worse place than the one from which she began. The solution to this problem, according to Abba Serapion, is simply to remember that the victory over sin belongs to God, and not to the victorious Christian.

This remembrance of the work of God in overcoming vice and sin is central to the life of humility. In remembering that only God liberates the Christian to virtue, a person sets himself aside in much the same way that he does when he follows the counsels of the elders rather than the judgments of his own mind. Ultimately, humility in the *Conferences* amounts to a pouring out of the self in order that all judgments of the mind, and all credit for attaining virtue, may be replaced by God's wisdom, and credit given to God. Indeed, when a monk submits himself to the elders it is not ultimately mere human beings in the desert who become his guides, but rather God working through those who, by way of their own humility, have come to be guided by God. In much the same way, the Christian who credits God's grace for conquering sin is guided in all things by God, and never by his own mind. In humility, the Christian's own capacity for personal judgment and self-congratulation will atrophy over time as she becomes so accustomed to following the guidance of God that she becomes incapable of walking any other path. In such a state, the Christian will by definition also have attained the fullness of discernment and discretion, because God cannot but guide the Christian to truth. Through the execution of such discretion and discernment, the Christian will, in turn, find herself living out the life of balance that is necessary for purity of heart.

These, then, are the prime virtues that the Christian seeks. As we have noted, this is not an exhaustive list of all the possible virtues, nor is it even an account of every virtue discussed in St John Cassian's writings specifically. Indeed, in the remainder of this book we will bring up a few of the many other virtues discussed in the *Conferences* as each becomes important in a given chapter. These include, for instance, charity, compassion, chastity, and patience. As we have already noted, these relational virtues are better treated in subsequent chapters.

We should make special note that also on the list of virtues that we will treat later on is love. I draw this fact out especially because it may be somewhat surprising. After all, love is of the utmost importance in scripture, prayer, and all of Christian life. It is one of the defining characteristics of purity of heart, as we have seen, and it is frequently presented (including by the *Conferences*) as the greatest of all Christian virtues. However, our choice not to class love as a primary virtue for discussion here does not reflect any low place of importance. Rather it simply reflects the fact that love is something that is directed to others, or to God. It is a relational category once again. Therefore, it will be better to define Christian love explicitly in chapter two (our discussion of lay life in society).

Theoria

Theoria, often translated as "contemplation," is a critical concept for most of the ancient fathers of the Church, and it is important for us to talk about it right away. Coming into true contemplation, *theoria,* is, according to the *Conferences,* the essential purpose of a monk's life. According to Abba Moses, *theoria* is a state of mind in which the monk contemplates "only the vision of God."[41] We may thus define it as the transcendent and total experience of God that is commonly referred to by many later fathers as the vision of divine light. In true *theoria,* the Christian proceeds through contemplative prayer to become conscious of nothing but God, establishing a direct connection with the divine that she inevitably fails to describe in words.

As we have already seen in the teachings of Abba Moses, there is little or no meaningful distinction between God himself and the kingdom of God in the thought of the *Conferences.* As such, *theoria,* since it amounts to a complete and total connection of the

[41]   *Conf.* I.VIII.3.

mind with God, is, in turn, a mental experience in this life of the kingdom of God itself. It is thus a means by which the monk receives a foretaste of his *telos* while still awaiting its fullness. For the fathers of the *Conferences*, *theoria* is the most profound such human experience of the kingdom of God that is possible for those still alive in the fallen flesh. It is therefore no surprise that Abba Moses calls *theoria* the chiefest good for Christians.

> You can see, then, that the Lord has established *theoria* (that is, divine contemplation) as the principal good. Thus, we understand the other virtues to be of the second order (granted, they are necessary and useful and good), since every one of them is done in order to realize this one purpose. Indeed, the Lord says "you are worried and troubled by many things, yet only a few are needful—or, really, one" [Lk 10.41]. Thus, he locates the greatest good not in practical, laudable works that bear many fruits, but in the contemplation of the Lord himself: one thing—simple.[42]

For Abba Moses, the point of practicing virtues is eventually to arrive at the contemplation of the kingdom of God in *theoria*. This is true to so great a degree that there is even a sense in which virtues become potential impediments to the ultimate good in that they can distract a monk from the work of contemplation. Thus teaches Abba Theonas in the twenty-third conference.

> So, while all of the virtues that I have discussed are good and precious things in themselves, still they pale in comparison to the brilliance of *theoria*. Indeed, they often drag the saints away and cut them off from that sublime contemplation, doing so by way of earthly concerns (albeit, often including good works).[43]

The Christian focus on virtue and good works, according to Abba Theonas, must not exceed its place such as to become an impediment to the total devotion of the mind to God alone that is contemplation.

---

42   *Conf.* I.VIII.2–3.
43   *Conf.* 23.IV.4.

In spite of this fact, it is impossible for any person to remain in this most contemplative state while still living in the flesh of this world, as Abba Theonas himself also notes. One must eventually tend to the needs of the body, if nothing else.

> Even among the most preeminent of all just and holy people, who do you suppose—while still in the shackles of this body—could possibly hold on to this highest good to the point of never ceasing in divine contemplation, not for a minute drawn by earthly thoughts away from him who alone is good?[44]

The implied answer to Abba Theonas' question is "no one." Yet the fathers of the *Conferences* nonetheless seek out what moments of *theoria* are possible for them at every turn. For them, contemplation is time spent in the kingdom of God, and, as we noted in the beginning of this chapter, it is the kingdom of God that is the *telos* of the Christian.

We will not bring up *theoria* again as a subject of direct inquiry until chapter five, but it is important to discuss it here because of what the fathers' approach to *theoria* tells us about the nature of the Christian *telos*. For the fathers of the *Conferences*, the Christian alive in this world can, in principle, attain to a taste of her real *telos* for a time—an experience of what is her promised destiny if she seeks purity of heart. To experience the kingdom is not something that awaits Christians *only* at the end of time (though it does so await us), it is also something that can become a present reality at least to a degree. It is for this reason that the fathers of the *Conferences* valued *theoria* so highly, and that they understood the practice of virtue as preparing the way for *theoria* in just the same way that purity of heart prepares one for the kingdom of God.

As we continue our exploration of how the wisdom of the *Conferences* can be applied in lay life, we will need to maintain an awareness of how really present the fathers believed the kingdom could be to us here and now. This is especially because *theoria*, as we will see, is not the only profound experience foreshadowing the

---

[44] *Conf.* 23.V.3.

kingdom that can arise from virtue. Purity of heart makes way for all manner of holy experiences of our *telos*, and we will talk about some of them in the chapters to come.

Means to the End

Here is how things stand so far. We have observed the five most important virtues through which the fathers in the *Conferences* teach us to establish the purity of heart that is the goal of Christian life. These are detachment, discernment, discretion, balance, and humility. We have observed that the fathers taught Christians to practice these virtues in order to guide them to their proper *telos*, which is the kingdom of God. We have noted that this *telos* can be tasted to some extent in this life, and is most fully so tasted in the experience of *theoria* according to the fathers. We have finally alluded to further experiences of this kind of foretaste of the kingdom. All this vocabulary of the Christian goal and *telos*, along with our identification of the virtues, will serve us well in the discussions to come, as it will allow us to be specific about how life in the world can facilitate the accomplishment of the purpose of Christian life. The teachings we have discussed so far apply to all Christians whether in the world or monastic, whether laity or clergy. We will now speak briefly about the fundamental nature of what *differentiates* a monk and a Christian living in the world.

In working toward their goal and *telos*, the monks of the desert employed a wide range of religious practices with which most Orthodox Christians are already familiar. In a passage quoted above, Abba Moses presents an excellent summary list of the particular activities that define the life of the monk over and against other forms of Christian life. These are solitude, fasts, vigils, labors, asceticism, readings, and other virtuous things.[45] He notes that every one of these definitive practices is done for the pursuit of purity of heart. The *Conferences* go into plenty of detail regarding the nature of these practices, how monks should carry them out, and their

---

[45]   *Conf.* I.VII.I.

various risks and rewards, though we will not discuss these details here. Suffice it to say that pursuits that fall into these seven basic categories of activity are what, according to the *Conferences,* give the life of the monk its outward form.

It is important to see, however, that for Abba Moses and the other fathers of the *Conferences,* these activities, which mark off the life of the monk, are always negotiable means to an end, never to be pursued for themselves.

> If some earnest and necessary undertaking prevents us from carrying out our regular disciplines, we must stay clear of any sadness, anger or indignation [in response]. The whole purpose of the practices we neglected was to set such things aside! No— the gain of fasting does not measure up to the loss of anger, nor is the fruit born of reading on par with the harm of contempt for a brother. Those things which are of secondary importance, such as fasting, vigils, withdrawal from the world, and meditation on scripture, we ought to practice with a view to our main object, namely purity of heart, which is love.[46]

For Abba Moses, a man certainly cannot be a monk without the solitude, vigils, fasts and the like—but the pursuit of these practices is never his purpose as a Christian.

This being the case, we may now make an important observation. According to the fathers of the *Conferences,* what makes a monk a monk is ultimately *not* what is most fundamental about Christian life. What defines a monk is, instead, the particulars of the secondary practices in which he engages in pursuit of the fundamental (and universal) goal and *telos* of all Christians. A monk is what he is because of the tools that he uses in his quest for purity of heart, not because only he pursues this in the first place. In fact, Abba Serenus goes so far as to say that life in the desert not only does not inherently lead to holiness, but in fact only shows to the monk what he has failed to become.

[46]   *Conf.* I.VII.1–3.

> The progress of time (and the life of solitude) that you might
> expect would bring about the perfection of our inner man, has
> only done this for us: we have realized what we cannot be. It has
> not made us into what we are trying to become.[47]

Here Abba Serenus makes his point in stark terms. There is
nothing about the life of a monk in the desert that leads auto-
matically to holiness. The incidentals of this life ever remain only
that—incidental.

Moreover, for the fathers of the *Conferences*, not even every monk
can pursue the same kind of lifestyle. There are various forms of
monasticism, each appropriate to different individuals, as Abba
Abraham notes in the twenty-fourth conference.

> While being a hermit is a good thing, we do not recommend it
> as suitable for everyone; for a lot of people it is ineffective, or
> even downright destructive. In the same vein, while we agree that
> the way of life of monks in a monastery—and caring for one's
> brothers—is holy and honorable, still we do not think that it
> ought to be pursued by everyone. And, again, there is tremendous
> benefit in giving hospitality, but it is not possible for everyone to
> do it without doing damage to his patience.[48]

Abba Abraham, like the other fathers of the *Conferences*, is attentive
to the differences between individuals pursuing the Christian life,
including those who are monks and nuns. People have different
needs in their pursuit of purity of heart.

As a result of the inherent differences between individuals
within the Church, the fathers of the *Conferences* teach that individual Christians must acknowledge and seize the particular
spiritual opportunities that are present to them. Abba Paphnutius
notes that it would be strange if things were any other way.

> Your objection would be on target if every work or discipline
> had only a beginning and an end, with no middle between them.
> Yet, we know that God uses many different methods of salvation,

---

[47]   *Conf.* 7.III.1.
[48]   *Conf.* 24.VII.3.

and we, in turn, attend more or less diligently to them—these opportunities granted by the divine.[49]

Thus, every individual Christian must find her place within the Church, and pursue her path with zeal and strength, as Abba Nesteros teaches.

> Therefore it is useful and appropriate that a man struggle with great commitment and diligence to attain perfection in the work he has begun, in accordance with the purpose that he seeks or the grace he has received. Though he might praise and admire the virtues of others, he returns again and again to his own monastic commitment, knowing that, according to the apostle, the body of the Church is one, though its members are many [Rom 12.4–5].[50]

Indeed, so important is it for the individual to find her right place within the Church that Abba Daniel even argues that the state of the souls of outright pagans simply living for the world is, in fact, better than that of the Christian monk who has wrongly estimated himself, and thus improperly pursued the monastic life and fallen into a lukewarm state.

> The carnal man (i.e. the worldly man and the pagan) is more readily brought to saving conversion and to the heights of perfection than one who has been professed as a monk, but has not, as his rule directs, laid hold on the way of perfection, and so has once for all drawn back from that fire of spiritual fervor. For the former is at least broken down by the sins of the flesh, and acknowledges his uncleanness, and in his compunction hastens from carnal pollution to the fountain of true cleansing, and the heights of perfection.[51]

In the wrong hands, the tools of the monk are even less effective for salvation than the pain of worldly sin itself!

For the fathers of the *Conferences,* then, the tools for seeking purity of heart and the kingdom are many, but not all are right for

---

[49]   *Conf.* 3.XII.1.
[50]   *Conf.* 14.V.1.
[51]   *Conf.* 4.XIX.4. Translation adapted from Gibson.

all people. Teachings like those of Abba Daniel, quoted immediately above, cannot but call us to consider very seriously which of
these tools of salvation are those to which we are called, lest we
become lukewarm in whatever pursuit we choose and find ourselves
worse off than those who are not even trying to live a Christian
life. There is a clear sense among the fathers that every individual
Christian must know and understand his or her place within the
Church, and pursue that particular Christian life whole-heartedly.
For the monk, this is the life of solitude and asceticism, lived either
in the desert or in a monastery.

For the lay person, however, this is a life lived not in the desert,
and not within the walls of a convent, but in the world. And so we
have arrived at the crux of our discussions in this chapter. What
we are seeking to understand in the chapters that will follow is the
nature of the tools for seeking the universal Christian goal and *telos*
that are properly suited for implementation by those who are called
to live in the world. Where the *Conferences* discuss the tools of the
monk in great detail, we will explore the tools of the lay person
instead, building on the teachings of the *Conferences* and grounding
our discussion in them all the while. Often, we will discover that
the monk and the layman find themselves in a very similar position regarding their pursuit of purity of heart, and that certain
tools of the monk are similar or identical to those best employed
by a person in the world. Yet, we will also often find that what
is demanded (and what is offered) by worldly life is substantially
different from what is demanded (or offered) by monastic life.
What is more, we will at times note that practices engaged by the
monk and non-monastic alike may be similar outwardly, yet have a
different purpose or meaning in each context. In discussing all this,
we seek to be true to the teachings of the *Conferences*, which demand
that we understand the specific path in front of us in order that we
may walk it with vigor and find, at its end, purity of heart leading
to the kingdom of God.

All Things Working for Salvation

We conclude this chapter by presenting some assurance that what we are seeking to do as lay people—namely, to pursue purity of heart—really can be done *through* life in the world. We require such an assurance simply because life in the world can often seem terribly ill-suited to the pursuit of our goal and *telos*. For instance, we may ask, how is one to develop discretion and discernment in a world full of false teachers pulling us in every direction—even sometimes within the Church? Or how are we to cultivate humility in a world that does not merely encourage, but that utterly relies on pride as a means for driving all human activity? Or how are we to seek detachment in a world of such rampant materialism?

Indeed, these questions grow out of some of the greatest problems of life in the world—precisely the kinds of obstacles to virtue that have caused so many faithful Christians to become monks and nuns over the centuries. Seeking a path to God more free from some of these challenges, these men and women have chosen to pursue separation from the world, rather than drive forward into the complex and frightful questions we are raising here. Indeed, there is nothing wrong with us pining a little for a vision of a life that, like theirs, is rather more free from these things; to feel some longing for the monastic choice demonstrates that we recognize the challenges of the world for the serious problems that they are. Yet, even if we do so pine for a monastery or hermitage now and then, we remain people in the world.

In light of this, it is important to keep in mind that the *Conferences* teach that, if we take the correct approach, any challenge or blessing can and must become a tool for our salvation. In other words, absolutely anything we encounter or experience in our lives as Christians can become an opportunity to seek greater purity of heart if we know how to approach it rightly. The following quotation is from Abba Theodore in the sixth conference.

> All those things, then, which are considered fortunate, and are
> described as those "on the right hand," which the holy apostle

designates [in 2 Cor 6.7–10] by the terms honor and good report; and those, too, which are counted misfortunes, which [Paul] clearly means by dishonor and evil report, and which he describes as "on the left hand," become to the perfect man "the armor of righteousness," if, when they are brought upon him, he bears them bravely: because, as he fights with these, and uses those very weapons with which he seems to be attacked, and is protected by them as by bow and sword and stout shield against those who bring these things upon him, he secures the advantage of his patience and goodness, and obtains a grand triumph of steadfastness by means of those very weapons of his enemies which are hurled against him to kill him—if only he is not elated by success or cast down by failure, but ever marches straightforward on the royal road, and does not swerve from that state of tranquility as it were to the right hand, when joy overcomes him, nor let himself be driven so to speak to the left hand, when misfortune overwhelms him, and sorrow holds sway.[52]

For Abba Theodore, the fortunes of life, whatever they may be, all become tools of salvation in the hands of those who are pursuing purity of heart, if they walk the royal road of balance with virtue. In the chapters to come, we will discuss the lay person's relationship to society, family, property, work, and religious life. As we explore these topics, we will continually ask how our experiences in these spheres can become the tools for the pursuit of purity of heart that Abba Theodore implies that they can be.

Finally, a few words of simple comfort. The same Abba Theodore whom we have just quoted reminds us of God's promise that "there is much peace for those who love [God's] name, and for them there is no stumbling block."[53] What should we make of this? Quite simply, it teaches us that our task as Christians is daunting, but that we take it on with the full assurance that it is possible to walk the hard road of life—wherever we live it—in peace, if we seek purity of heart and the kingdom. There can be no such

---

[52]   *Conf.* 6.IX.3. Translation adapted from Gibson.
[53]   Quoted in *Conf.* 6.IX.3.

thing as an impossible impediment to our goal and *telos* if we truly seek God. This we must constantly remember in the face of the profound struggle that life in the world is for us as Christians.

CHAPTER 2

Society

*Love has been perfected among us in this: that we may have boldness in the day of
judgement; because as he is, so are we in this world.*
1 John 4.17

In many ways the word "society" serves to summarize most or
all of that which a non-monastic Christian encounters on a daily
basis, but which a desert monk seeks to avoid as a general rule. This
includes constant interaction with other human beings, as well as
direct engagement in their complex social structures, economies,
politics, and the like. It would obviously be a mistake to assume
that any monks, including the fathers of the *Conferences*, are cut off
from such concerns completely. Far from it! When they were not
themselves forced to go into the world at times, the fathers found
society constantly coming to them by way of pilgrims and visitors.
Reading the *Conferences*, one sees that the desert fathers knew well
the goings-on of their time, and indeed affected them at the very
least through their prayers, and often in direct ways as well. Yet the
monks of the *Conferences* do seek to minimize their interactions
with society and maximize their time of solitude. This basic, if
imperfect, separation from society is one defining characteristic of
a monk. Conversely, lay Christians engage society head-on, finding
at most a few moments a day in which to set aside the cares of the
world. Essential to the call of the lay person, then, is the decision
to embrace a full, if occasionally hesitant, engagement with society.
In this chapter we will explore some of the ways that such an engagement can and should become a tool for salvation.

If we are to draw any wisdom at all from the *Conferences* on this point, though, we need first to sharpen our way of thinking about society somewhat. While it is by no means the case that socially constructed realities (such as economies, nation-states and the like) are unimportant, the teachings of the *Conferences* hardly ever really address these kinds of topics. Even if they did, the texts from the *Conferences* are ancient enough now that much of what they might say would be unlikely to apply very well to Christian life today. What the *Conferences* do talk a lot about, however, is human relationships.

Relationships are the basic material out of which society is built. As mind-boggling as the task would be, a truly exhaustive description of any society would need to include an account of every interaction between every person within it. We cannot be without the broad categories that we use to discuss these relationships in groups (categories like "corporation," "political movement," or "nation") but every such group is composed of people and their relationships. The fathers of the *Conferences* are therefore most helpful to our thinking about society if we do this thinking in terms of the relationships that make it up, in other words, at an atomic level.

We will focus, then, on society as a network of relationships. We can break down these relationships into two broad categories. First are those that we will call "direct relationships." By this we mean those that exist between ourselves and everyone with whom we are acquainted personally (and thus have probably met face to face), from our friends, to co-workers, to those we meet on the street or at the store, to neighbors, to anyone else who happens to be around us. The second category comprises what we will call "mediated relationships." These are relationships that we have with people whom we do not really know personally. These can be people like government officials, other voters, people in the media, journalists, entertainers, or even other drivers on the road—anyone we might connect with through various forms of media, hear about in the news or merely see from a distance without meeting.

Mediated relationships have a very different character from direct relationships, as we all know intuitively. They tend to be more fragmented and disembodied. We are often less patient with people in our mediated relationships, more willing to judge them or lionize them, more capable of seeing their actions and character in black and white. Yet, they remain relationships. They are connection points between people, as weak and distorted a picture as they might give us of the other person at times.

It will be our basic assumption in this chapter that transforming life in society into a tool for salvation is best begun by transforming the individual relationships, both direct and mediated, that make up our connection with society. In short, every relationship we as Christians have, no matter how close or distant, must become a tool for salvation.

This chapter is divided into four sub-sections, followed by some concluding remarks. In the first section on "Cultivating Love, Assuaging Anger" we will assess the goal of life in society by explicating the image of the ideal Christian relationship that is presented in the *Conferences*. We will frame genuine Christian love, which, as we will see, is a relational form of purity of heart, as the key goal to which we strive as lay people in the world. In the remaining three sections, we will explore three of the most important ways in which life in society can help us to cultivate such love and therefore purity of heart. Society does so especially by offering opportunities for charity and good works, compassion, and patience—sections two through four in order. Finally, throughout the chapter we will see that if the Christian is able to exercise discretion and develop an awareness of her shortcomings in relation to society, even the failure of love can itself become a spiritual opportunity.

The Goal of Life in Society: Cultivating Love, Assuaging Anger

Because we are exploring life in society as a web of relationships, it is important to establish from the outset a picture of what the fathers of the *Conferences* thought relationships should be like for

Christians. No matter how deep into the desert they went, none of the fathers was under any illusion that a human being can live free from relationships with others. What is more, the fathers did not consider a life of absolute solitude, totally cut off from anyone else permanently, to be particularly appealing. Human beings, they seem to assume, require at least a small level of contact with others for their basic spiritual health. Thus, the fathers of the *Conferences* engage in a substantial amount of straightforward discussion about human relationships. The most extended such discussion occupies all of the sixteenth conference, delivered by Abba Joseph on the topic of friendship. Our first task here is to present a summary of his teaching on the ideal for Christian relationships, namely friendships built on Christian love (a term that we will define in a moment), along with the key impediment that derails them from this ideal, namely, anger (the opposite of love).

Abba Joseph presents his definition of Christian love near the start of the conference. He begins by assessing a few of the different kinds of close human relationships that exist in the world, emphasizing especially relationships between family members, and those between people who associate for various necessary pursuits, for example, business partners. For Abba Joseph, these kinds of human associations are perfectly normal and good—but they are fundamentally relationships of necessity that can often fall short of the ideal of love. In explaining this, he defines love nicely.

> One sort of love, in particular, is insoluble. This is that love that is founded not on the basis of a recommendation, or some office, or great largess, or a business contract, or natural necessity, but only on mutual similarity in virtue. This love, I say, is not sundered by any turn of events; long distance and the march of time cannot prevail to erode or destroy such love. And not only that—even death itself cannot rend it. This is the true and unwavering affection that forms out of the perfection and virtue that is mirrored between the friends.[1]

---

[1]   *Conf.* 16.III.1–2.

Real love, according to this passage, is not any feeling of admiration, nor dependence. We may add that, by extension, it is not some sense of fondness or emotional warmth, nor is it the acceptance of another person without criticism, nor is it a protective instinct for a family member, nor is it by any means a romantic feeling. Instead, for Abba Joseph, real Christian love is nothing more and nothing less than that which arises from a devotion to virtue shared between two friends.

If, then, we import the language that we used in chapter one in our discussion of the goal and *telos* of Christian life, we see that Abba Joseph is teaching here that genuine Christian love amounts to a shared pursuit of purity of heart. We can conclude this because, as we know, purity of heart and the real fullness of virtue are one and the same thing. Thus, genuine Christian love is purity of heart made mutual and binding between two human beings. It is what arises when two individuals commit themselves to the pursuit of this goal together, and thus begin to keep one another aflame like logs in a fire that burn bright in one another's presence, but can scarcely stay lit at all when alone. Real love is the yoke that brings together two people onto a single path if and when that path is purity of heart, and its destination the kingdom of God.

The passage that we just quoted makes evident that for Abba Joseph, the ideal human relationship is simply a relationship of this kind of love. Through love, two people strengthen one another in their holy pursuit of their Christian goal, and in so doing, their bond becomes indestructible, he says, to the point that "neither a divergence in what they desire, nor a quarrel will break it."[2] To establish a relationship so constituted on genuine love is, for him, to create a Christian friendship.

Abba Joseph now expands on his teaching by identifying six key foundations for this kind of true friendship. 1) Detachment with regard to all earthly possessions and wealth. 2) Not considering oneself wise, but deferring to the point of view of the other.

---

[2]   *Conf.* 16.III.2.

3) Seeking love and peace above all. 4) Refraining from anger at
all times. 5) Calming the anger of the friend should it arise. 6)
Constant reflection on the coming of death.[3] There are strong
parallels here between the foundations of a friendship and the key
virtues that we identified in chapter one as central to the pursuit of
purity of heart. In particular, one notices Abba Joseph's emphasis
on detachment, as well as mutual deferral to one another of the
sort that is foundational to discernment, discretion, humility, and
balance. The presence of these parallels between the virtues that
lead to purity of heart and those that are necessary for friendship,
of course, is unsurprising in light of what Abba Joseph understands genuine love to be. Love is nothing other than the sharing
of a commitment to virtue, and so it is naturally the most essential
virtues that build up a friendship of love. Conversely, where virtue
is absent, love, which is shared virtue, cannot be, and so, as Abba
Joseph says, "the perfect love of friendship cannot endure except
between perfect men of identical virtue."[4]

Much more could be said about Abba Joseph's understanding
of friendship as a topic in itself, but our purpose here, instead, is
to explore Christian life in society. In what way does Abba Joseph's
teaching bear upon that discussion? The answer is that the kind
of friendship built on love that Abba Joseph presents as ideal here
is, in essence, the ideal kind of relationship that is to be sought
between ourselves and every human being that we encounter in
the world. Everyone in the world, from strangers to acquaintances
to friends, presents—in theory—an opportunity to begin a real
friendship. Abba Joseph himself notes as much by saying that such
love (which he refers to with the Greek term *agape*) can be shown
to everyone.[5] This is so even in our mediated relationships for, as
Abba Joseph says, "with God, it is the convergence of wills, not of
location, that brings brothers under one roof."[6]

[3]   *Conf.* 16.IV.1–3.
[4]   *Conf.* 16.V.1.
[5]   *Conf.* 16.XIV.1.
[6]   *Conf.* 16.III.5.

Our goal through life in society, then, is to transform all of our relationships in the world into real Christian friendships—sites of genuine love. This is not to say, however, that we should actually expect to get anywhere close to reaching this goal. Even among our dearest friends, we can probably count a small handful of people (if any at all) with whom we share even a shadow of the kind of total love and mutual devotion to purity of heart that Abba Joseph describes. He, however, is entirely aware of this problem, and for this reason he spends virtually all of his time in the sixteenth conference discussing the reasons for which human relationships *fail* to become what they are meant to be. For him, the essential thing that breaks down relationships of all sorts is anger. Because most of our relationships in society do not even begin to approach Abba Joseph's ideal, understanding his teaching on anger is critical for trying to begin the work of moving these relationships toward their goal.

For Abba Joseph, anger is to be avoided by Christians at all costs.

> For nothing is greater than love, and, conversely, nothing is worse than fury and anger. Indeed, anything—no matter how useful and necessary it seems—ought to be left aside, if doing this will avoid riling up anger.[7]

Abba Joseph teaches that a Christian's first priority is to prevent anger from arising in a relationship. By this teaching, Abba Joseph does not mean simply that we should avoid open conflict with other people, which is to say, avoid anger's most obvious outward symptoms. Indeed, pretending one has ceased to be angry by doing things like isolating oneself, stewing in silence, or being what we moderns might describe as "passive aggressive" and trying to silently provoke others is, for Abba Joseph, a sign that a person's anger has not really been addressed and alleviated.[8] Instead of being satisfied with such behaviors, the Christian seeking a friendship based on

---

[7] *Conf.* 16.VII.1.
[8] *Conf.* 16.XV–XX.

genuine love will seek always to earnestly let go of any anger that might arise, doing so on the level of her inner self. Only in this way will she wholly remove the "first cause—dissension, which is born mostly out of fallen and earthly things."[9]

Anger, then, must be eradicated from the inner man if friendship is to grow. Abba Joseph offers some advice on how to do this. For him, the ability of a person to let go his or her anger can be cultivated especially by the exercise of discretion, one of the key virtues we discussed in chapter one. The Christian, even when genuinely wronged by another person, must call her mind to the kind of love that she knows can exist between two people devoted to virtue.

> First, a monk who has been struck by any kind of injustice ought to maintain his tranquility—not just that of his lips, but that of his heart—to the very depths.... Nor, stewing in his present state, should he bring up the things that his seething anger and his irritated mind suggest in the heat of the moment. Instead, he should recall the gift of his former love, and picture in his mind the renewal of peace.... Thus he will fulfill these words of the prophet: "in wrath remember mercy" [Heb 3.2].[10]

Ultimately, to turn our minds immediately to the thought of Christian love whenever we are angry is to begin to make manifest that very quality of love, and doing so chases anger out of the soul at its very outset. What is more, it transforms moments of anger into motivations toward anger's complete opposite, namely, love. Instead of an impediment to Christian friendship, anger that is met with discretion becomes a spur to love, and thus a tool in the pursuit of purity of heart.

This point is very important because, in concert with the words of the other three most recently quoted passages, it implies something critical about Abba Joseph's understanding of anger. For

---

[9]   *Conf.* 16.IX. Abba Joseph acknowledges that among Christians anger can also have a second cause, this being disagreement over spiritual or religious questions.
[10]   *Conf.* 16.XXVI.2.

him, anger and love exist within a mutually exclusive dichotomy. They cannot overlap one another, and cannot take up the same space within the Christian soul at the same time. Where anger is present, love is absent, and vice versa. This is why, for Abba Joseph, to bring the thought of genuine Christian love to mind through discretion pushes out anger as a direct consequence.

> And so your mind, expanded by long-suffering and patience, will have within it a space for healthy reflection, in which the acrid smoke of your anger (however it has been received and accumulated) can be diffused.[11]

Here, Abba Joseph is counseling that in the mind that has deliberately created a space for love, anger is immediately swallowed by that love when the two meet. The greater the space in the mind devoted to love, the fewer places there are for anger to take root and grow.

In light of this, perhaps the best way for us to think about Abba Joseph's teaching on love and anger is to picture human beings as creatures whose minds constantly reside somewhere between two distant poles, moving backward and forward. These poles are anger and love. As the mind moves toward love, it moves away from anger, and vice versa. The mind, moreover, can never direct itself to both at once—it must constantly choose which to pursue in every moment of every relationship. There is no doubt about which state Abba Joseph thinks we ought to seek.

All of Abba Joseph's teachings so far probably make pretty good sense to most readers. As much as we may not live up to the ideal of mutual purity of heart, which defines real love, it is pretty easy to see its value, and it is equally easy to see the direct opposition to this ideal that anger presents within us. Yet, one of the most provocative aspects of Abba Joseph's teaching on relationships is that he does not hold the Christian responsible *only* for his own personal inner state in relationship, but demands that every person be responsible also for the anger of other people. Christians,

---

[11]   *Conf.* 16.XXVII.2.

according to him, must put their all into trying to assuage the anger of anyone who might be offended at them, for good reasons or for bad.

> For the one who said that you must not be angry with another, said also that you must not ignore another person's heartache. Between destroying yourself and someone else, there exists no distinction in the eyes of the God "who desires that all men be saved" [1 Tim 2.4].[12]

Abba Joseph is unrelenting on this point, to the degree that he sometimes appears to place total responsibility for the anger of others on the shoulders of the person toward whom it is directed. He even says that those who refuse to try and cool such anger will be punished by God as though they had committed the sin of anger themselves.[13] It would be natural for us to consider this teaching a bit extreme. After all, there is always a point at which nothing can be done to avert the choice of another person to be angry. However, while there is no sense in which Abba Joseph expects that the Christian should always be able to *succeed* in cooling the anger of another, he does always expect that one will *try* to do so, really taking that anger upon himself as though it were his own.

Thus, Abba Joseph presents human relationships as contact points between two individuals whose attitude toward one another wavers between the poles of love and anger. What is more, he places responsibility for the state of *both* parties in a particular relationship on the shoulders of the Christian. Ultimately, we as Christians seek to make all of our relationships of all varieties into Christian friendships built on genuine love both by seeking to change our own inner state, and by taking responsibility for the state of other people in those relationships.

Given the nature of love and anger in relationships as defined by Abba Joseph, doing this involves four basic kinds of effort. First, we do whatever we can to assuage anger within ourselves. Second

---

12   *Conf.* 16.VI.7.
13   *Conf.* 16.VI.7.

we do what is possible to assuage anger in other people. Third, we do what we can to promote love within ourselves. Fourth, we do what we can to promote love in other people. In so doing, we seek to push the soul of both parties in all of our relationships toward the pole of Christian love, and thus to make them relationships in which that love is shared, which is to say to transform them into real Christian friendships. This means that we are seeking to turn every relationship we have with everyone everywhere into a site where purity of heart is mutually sought with absolute maximal effort on both sides.

Now, it is probably hard to imagine buying a cup of coffee and finding ourselves lifted toward purity of heart by our instantaneous connection in Christian love with the cashier. It is just as hard to imagine reading the news and realizing the same love in light of what the politicians have been up to that week. Indeed, it is hard even to imagine simply not getting angry when that same cashier gets our order wrong, or when those same politicians act as politicians do—and we may find it impossible even to conceive of becoming capable of preventing them from returning such anger upon us. Yet, if we are going to seek purity of heart while living in the world, nothing less is expected of us, because it is only when we do these things that we allow purity of heart to grow in and through our contact with other human beings.

So, how do we really work toward a goal so distant? We have already made mention of the importance of discretion as a tool for casting away anger in ourselves, and we should keep this tool in mind as we proceed. In the next three sections, we will discuss some of the other primary tools presented in the *Conferences* for cultivating and seeking to spread genuine love, and thus real purity of heart, by way of our relationships with others in society.

Charity and Good Works

Perhaps the most obvious spiritual opportunity offered to us by society is that of performing good works. This opportunity is, in fact, so obvious that we will only devote a very short section to it here, and thus the length of this section is in inverse proportion to the significance of charity and good works in the Christian life. As for the subject, we will pay particular attention to acts of charity, taken as a broad category. That is to say that by "charity" we refer to situations in which we as Christians give something of ourselves, our resources, or our time to benefit others in needs. Such charity may be directed toward anyone in society, certainly including the poor, but also those around us who need help in one way or another at any given time.

The idea that doing good to other people is an important, indeed a necessary, component of Christian life is so central to the *Conferences* that it is rarely addressed explicitly. While the monks of the *Conferences* see the Gospels as documents rich in profound spiritual mysteries that run much deeper than the surface meaning of a given passage, they equally see the teachings of Jesus on subjects like clothing the naked and feeding the hungry as simple and direct commands.

In at least one passage from the first conference, however, St John and St Germanus bring up the topic of charity with some trepidation in their voices. Having heard Abba Moses extol the importance of *theoria* over all other virtues, the two travelers raise concerns that such a teaching runs contrary to the Lord's command to take up things like fasting, reading, mercy, hospitality and, indeed, charity.[14] Abba Moses, in his response, focuses on the importance of doing good works of charity, citing the Lord's teaching that whoever gives so much as a cup of water in his name will receive the reward of the kingdom.[15] One of the key reasons that St John records this discourse is probably in order to defend monasticism in principle. Objections to monasticism on the grounds that it is untrue to the gospels in being too removed from works of charity are heard frequently today, and it appears likely that they were familiar to St John as well. If so, it seems that he wanted to

---

[14]   Conf. I.IX.
[15]   Mt 10.42.

be sure, in the very first conference, to make clear that the monks of the desert were well aware of the importance of charity and capable of participating in it.

Beyond this rhetorical point, Abba Moses proceeds in his discourse on charity in a way that is helpful for us here. For him, charity is absolutely critical in the fallen world, but the Christian must recognize that it is necessary only *because* the world is fallen. Acts of charity matter now, but cannot be construed as ultimately of the highest importance because they will no longer be necessary (or even possible) in the new kingdom.

> As long, then, as this inequality lasts in this world, this sort of work will be needful and useful to the man that practices it, as it brings to a good purpose and a pious will the reward of an eternal inheritance: but it will come to an end in the life to come, where equality will reign, when there will be no longer inequality, on account of which these things must be done, but all men will pass from these manifold practical works to the love of God, and contemplation of heavenly things in continual purity of heart.[16]

It is interesting to note that Abba Moses explicitly identifies the improper distribution of earthly resources as the cause of poverty and human suffering in the world, pointing to greed as the source of this problem. His moral indictment of the unchecked accumulation of wealth is, if anything, all the more relevant today. More central to our discussion in this chapter, however, is Abba Moses' point that while works of charity will not be needed in the new kingdom, in the world as it exists here and now these works provide those already properly disposed toward God with an eternal reward. The implication is that acts of charity constitute a kind of final step taken by a person otherwise in good spiritual health—a capstone of their love for God.

The reason that Abba Moses sees good works in this way is implicit in another comment that he makes about the kind of spiritual transformation that is effected by various bodily works, including

---

[16] *Conf.* I.X.4. Translation Gibson.

the diligent reading of scripture, stern fasting, and, indeed, works of charity. All of these, he says, are made necessary only in the fallen world, but still are needed because one cannot attain to love without them.[17] Indeed, what good is there in developing an inward disposition of love toward God and humanity if such a disposition is not expressed by real charity toward others as well as by doing other things that make that love manifest? Love without outward acts of kindness is rather like an art museum that does not allow admittance to any visitors. Perhaps it is really there in some theoretical sense, but it is scarcely true to its real purpose.

Charity, then, is the natural outgrowth of a soul pursuing love over and against anger. When we are committed to love, we do good. Yet, charity is about more than the one giving it. The exercise of charity and good works is one of the most important means by which we take responsibility for the anger and brokenness of other people, and seek to guide them, and not just ourselves, toward genuine love in accordance with the teachings of Abba Joseph. To give of ourselves in love is to offer some solace, whether physical, emotional, or both, to another person in the world. It is to take responsibility for their spiritual state, and to act from this responsibility to better it. Acts of kindness of whatever sort are among the most concrete ways that we can contribute to another person's choosing love over anger. Thus, as much as good works, including forms of charity, can only exist in the fallen world, it is equally true that so long as the world *is* fallen, no Christian can be said to be pursuing purity of heart without doing them. They are not eternal, but they are critical.

Still, the contemplative life does remain more important, according to the fathers. They often mention the story of Martha and Mary from the Gospel of Luke as an illustration of this fact. Most readers are probably familiar with the tale of Mary sitting at the feet of Jesus, listening to his teaching, while Martha busies about in the kitchen, irritated that her sister is not helping. Jesus

[17]   *Conf.* I.X.3.

famously praises Mary for choosing the "better part," while not condemning Martha for her work of hospitality.[18] Abba Moses and many other fathers make it clear that the monks of the desert have chosen Mary as their chief example. For them, she represents a commitment to things like *theoria*, while Martha represents good works in the world. Christ's praise for Mary is, to them, an endorsement of their way of life without being a condemnation of charity and good works.

We may now make the essential observation of this brief section. As much as it is the case that those living in the world are practically certain to lack the amount of solitude necessary to pursue a life devoted chiefly to *theoria*, it is equally true that we who are surrounded constantly by other people have vastly more opportunities to express and develop our Christian love through acts of charity and kindness directed toward others. The *Conferences* remind us that we have indeed chosen the lesser part, in accordance with Jesus' words to Martha—but they do not teach that we have chosen the part of no use at all. In our engagement with the fleeting good that is a simple act of charity, we make actual whatever love we harbor in ourselves, and promote the same within others.

The converse is just as important to notice. In a world in which we are constantly surrounded by people in need, exercising discretion regarding our reactions to that need is a powerful tool for guiding us to the love that we are meant to harbor for all people. Each opportunity to do good shines a light on our inner state. What is our reaction to such moments? Do we find in our souls a bitterness and anger, or perhaps a hesitation to help? Or do we find an outpouring of love for other people—an eagerness to assist and do good as quickly and fully as possible? And, whatever our reaction, do we let opportunities for charity slip away from us?

It is almost certain that, at least at times, we do let good works go completely undone. Yet, even this, the culmination of a failure of love, tells us something of ourselves, and counsels us to return

---

[18] Lk 10.42.

to our pursuit of purity of heart. For, in passing by opportunities for acts of charity, we remind ourselves of our own lack of love, and thus our own complicity in anger. As we have seen, according to Abba Joseph, any simple recollection of the love that is possible between two human beings begins to make manifest that love, taking up the space within us that anger had occupied. Thus, acts of discretion regarding our responses to those in need replant the seed of love, which love we can again manifest in charity at the next opportunity—and so the cycle goes, if we will consent, upwards to God.

Part of Orthodox life in the world, then, must involve making the most of our overwhelmingly large opportunity to practice works of mercy, charity, and love. Not a day goes by for any of us that we are not accosted by a beggar, asked for help by a friend, or exposed to human suffering in the news—indeed, we probably have dozens of these experiences in the course of the average morning. Our material response to opportunities for charity may vary tremendously based on circumstances, but one thing cannot be questioned: we must react to every opportunity to offer mercy to another human being with an outpouring of love. At the very least, such an outpouring will always manifest itself as prayer, while at other times it may become material in the form of giving alms, doing volunteer work, making a phone call or visit to someone in need, or having a simple conversation with a lonely person. Such outpourings of love amount to both witnesses to and manifestations of its real presence in ourselves, and are, moreover, active attempts to begin repairing, on the side of another person, the anger that constitutes the essential brokenness of relationships.

The monks of the *Conferences* had many opportunities to offer acts of charity, mercy and love—but our opportunities as lay people in the world border on the infinite. To be true to the teachings of someone like Abba Moses, and the other fathers of the *Conferences*, we must begin to see society as a place in which we have the chance at almost any time of the day or night to offer acts of mercy and charity, and by so doing to "have our good intentions and pious will given over to the reward of the eternal inheritance."[19]

Compassion

As we have noted, the idea that charity and good works are important for Christians, and that life in the world offers a lot of opportunities to do them, is probably quite obvious. The work of developing compassion, however, which is the topic of this section, requires a little more discussion.

First, we should define the term "compassion" as we mean it here. While the modern English word tends to delineate a certain feeling of empathy or perhaps pity for another person, and a turning of heart toward mercy, its Latin root is somewhat less subtle and, in this case, it is the sense of the Latin that we wish to capture. The Latin root of "compassion" means "to bear with," or, "to suffer with," and the word can denote such co-suffering quite literally. To experience compassion is to undergo the same experiences and bear the same burdens as another person. For the Christian, it is to enter into the pain and spiritual shortcomings of their experience, bearing with them one yoke and one cross. Compassion is thus, in its basic form, a very simple act of the mind. It is a decision on the part of a person to suffer along with someone suffering, to simply cast himself as a compatriot to another rather than a bystander, enemy, or judge. Yet, as we will see in a moment, from such a simple mental act much is accomplished in our pursuit of Christian love.

In the *Conferences,* the fathers are fond of illustrating their points with stories from life. One of the most striking such tales comes from Abba Moses in the second conference and illustrates beautifully the importance of compassion. Abba Moses begins by making the point that not all elders in the desert are equally skilled in the arts of spiritual guidance, and that the old age of

[19] *Conf.* I.X.5.

a particular elder is not always a sure sign of his wisdom.[20] Some elders (Abba Moses actually says it is most of them) are lacking in the discernment and discretion necessary to guide other, younger monks on their quest for purity of heart.[21] Abba Moses tells the tale of one such unskilled elder. According to the story, a diligent young monk came to one of the elders in the desert to confess his feelings of impure sexual desire. Instead of offering advice and comfort about this common struggle, however, the elder monk berated the younger, and the young man left feeling hopeless and despairing.

Some time after, another elder of the desert, Abba Apollos, found the young man in his cell, broken with depression, and evidently gratifying himself sexually, having given up all hope of overcoming his passions. When Abba Apollos discovered what had happened, he sought to comfort the young monk and encouraged him to go back to struggling against the passions. The young man recovered and returned to his prayer and fasting.

After this, Abba Apollos prayed to God that the foolish elder might be taught a lesson by being allowed to be assaulted by the same kinds of thoughts that had troubled the young monk. Apollos' prayers were answered and the foolish elder was seen running out from his cell as if in madness, suddenly agonized with uncontrollable sexual thoughts prompted by demons. Abba Apollos offered the foolish elder some advice as well.

> "Return to your cell," said Apollos, "and finally recognize that until now you have been either ignored or dismissed by the devil rather than counted among those whom he attacks and with whom he wrangles every day, riled by their hard work and earnestness. Look at you—after persisting for so many years in this way of life, you were not able for a single day to look past just one of his darts fired in your direction—to say nothing about resisting it! This is why the Lord let you be wounded like this—so

---

[20]   We return to his comments to this end in our discussion of confession in chapter five, p. 170*ff*.
[21]   *Conf.* 2.XIII.1.

that, at least in your old age, you might learn to co-suffer in the weaknesses of others.[22]

There are two key points to observe here about Abba Apollos' comments. First, Abba Apollos assumes that the foolish elder's previous lack of temptation was a sign of the devil's lack of interest in him. As the quotation makes clear, the assumption on the part of the fathers of the *Conferences* is typically that those who are not disturbed by demons at least somewhat are not progressing very well spiritually. The idea is simply that the demons need not bother with those who are not drawing any closer to God. As a result, here and throughout the *Conferences*, a lack of spiritual temptation is generally considered to be a very worrisome sign that a particular person may also be lacking spiritual progress. In light of this basic assumption, the implication of the above passage is that the foolish elder was, in fact, *less* spiritually advanced than the young man, and yet able to be arrogant about his own lack of disturbing thoughts. After so many years, how could the elder make such a mistake?

The answer to this question comes by way of our second observation about the above passage. Abba Apollos identifies the key problem with the foolish elder's treatment of the young monk as arising from the elder's lack of compassion. In the case of the foolish elder, this lack of compassion led to him dispensing bad advice that nearly destroyed the spiritual life of a man suffering temptations. God's willingness to respond to Abba Apollos' prayers, and send temptation to the bad elder, was meant as a corrective to this problem, as Abba Apollos says.

And so, the purpose of this beneficial series of events has been realized; by them, the Lord meant to set that young man free from dangerous desires and to teach you something about the violence of their attack, and also about the feeling of compassion. As such, let us together implore him in prayer, that he may be pleased to

22   *Conf.* 2.XIII.9.

remove that goad with which he thought it right to strike you for your own good.[23]

The last line of Abba Apollos' words here illustrates that the bad elder's temptations are not, in themselves, a good thing, but that they have been meant to teach him about what he is lacking. In this case, Abba Apollos explicitly identifies this shortcoming as a lack of compassion. In short, the elder chose to sit in judgment of the young man rather than suffer along with him.

Yet, an outright miracle corrected the bad elder in the most powerful way imaginable. When Abba Apollos' prayer brought the same temptation upon the foolish elder as the young monk had suffered, the elder in that moment was forced by the power of God to experience the passions of the young man absolutely literally. He was thereby given an experience of the deepest form of compassion conceivable. He literally entered into the young monk's suffering and it became his own. This forced experience of co-suffering provided the foolish elder with a lesson in what compassion means, and why one cannot guide other monks without it.

While the character of the foolish elder in the story illustrates the profound risks of failing to engage other people with compassion, the figure of Abba Apollos provides an example of what is possible when one embraces it. By approaching the young monk with a desire to suffer his various temptations *with* him, Abba Apollos made possible a personal connection the results of which were love and encouragement for the young man, and a great lesson learned for the foolish elder. It is probably difficult for any of us to imagine the kind of spiritual tranquility and depth of love that must have been present in Abba Apollos for him to react to the young monk as he did. To walk in on a person actively engaged in masturbation (which the story strongly implies was what the young monk was up to) and to simply sit down to offer encouragement is probably beyond most of us. Yet, this is precisely what the situation demanded. Abba Apollos knew this because, when he saw the

---

[23]   *Conf.* 2.XIII.11.

young monk in his sin, his heart's first reaction was to suffer with him—to experience compassion in its Latin sense.

What, then, can we learn from the story about life in society? One of the most difficult problems faced in Christian life, and one that the desert monks experienced acutely, is the problem of our temptation to seek distance from the struggles of others, and to promote a sense of separation from the sins of the world around us. There is a certain passing resemblance to Christianity in doing so. Indeed, we certainly do not actively desire temptation for ourselves, nor do we approve of engaging in any sin. It might seem natural, on the surface, to seek distance from those struggling with such things—to set ourselves apart as more pure and more holy than others.

Yet, when we see ourselves as fundamentally different from other human beings, whether they are Christian or not, we quickly begin to resemble the foolish elder. We condemn and chastise those around us for their brokenness. Such condemnations and chastisements are, despite their outward claim to holiness, works of anger and never of love. If love is a shared commitment to purity of heart between individuals, then seeking separation from others, by its very nature, discourages love and can even make it ultimately impossible. To share the pursuit of purity of heart with another, one must share a connection with her, and in a fallen world, that means sharing a connection with a fallen person.

What is more, to see the sufferings of someone else provides another opportunity to live out the teachings of Abba Joseph on anger and love. In co-suffering compassion, we take on responsibility for the sin of other people quite literally—we accept it as our own, and so are naturally impelled to work toward its eventual healing. The distinction between the responsibility to others and the responsibility to oneself disappears, and all sin becomes our own sin. When we view other people this way, works of mercy that help them to heal from their own sins will flow easily, perhaps even miraculously, as they did for Abba Apollos. This, in turn, means that to find ourselves suffering what others suffer also means to find ourselves healed of this suffering whenever the other person is so healed. And because compassion itself is a powerful tool in effecting healing, its exercise therefore feeds back upon those who exhibit it within a relationship and begins to guide *both* parties to Christian love, and thus to the mutual pursuit of purity of heart. In short, compassion heals the compassionate person in the same instant as the sinner.

Perhaps most profound of all, however, is that if compassion involves accepting the sins of another as our own, then it equally involves inclusion in their repentance, should it come. By God's mercy, the foolish elder was forced to experience co-suffering and he learned from it to go back to repenting for those things that he pridefully thought he had overcome, but from which he still suffered. Such was the effect of a miracle in his case, but it should never have needed to come to that. The moment that the young monk walked into his cell, God had already provided the foolish elder with a golden opportunity to recognize his own sin manifest in another, and repent for it. Had he done so, he could have completely avoided the painful experience of being struck by temptation, while learning to set aside spiritual pride nonetheless. Instead, he refused to suffer along with the young monk. In an act of profound and exceptional mercy, God taught the foolish elder the same lesson anyway—but this time, it was taught by way of the stinging darts of temptation. How much more bitter a pedagogy?

Far from learning the hard way, like the bad elder, compassion invites us to repent of others' sins as though they were our own while skipping over the bitterness of sin itself. In the eleventh conference, Abba Chaeremon teaches this clearly.

> A person who, by such love, draws near to the image and likeness of God, will rejoice in the good because of the joy of the good itself. Possessing the same feeling of patience and gentleness, he will not be angered by the faults of sinners, but rather, sympathizing and co-suffering with their infirmities, he will ask for mercy on them. For he remembers that he was long opposed by

the impulses arising from similar passions until he was saved by
the mercy of the Lord.[24]

Most of us are accustomed to repenting for things that we have
done ourselves. Most of the time, this makes repentance a fairly
bitter pill to swallow as it is accompanied by a realization of our
own real guilt. Yet, compassion, as it was demonstrated by Abba
Apollos, provides the opportunity for a form of repentance, discussed here by Abba Chaeremon, that is not accompanied by a
feeling of personal guilt, but instead by an experience of inter-per-
sonal love. To repent in earnest for the sins of another is to turn
to God without requiring that we be stung by bitter arrows first.
Instead, we are invited by the sins of others to a repentance that
is both absolutely earnest, and full of *joy* rather than tears—joy
in mutual love meeting forgiveness. To repent in compassion is to
realize a moment in which mercy and peace kiss one another, in the
words of the psalm.

It is a great marvel indeed that a simple mental act of co-suffering could constitute so great a boon in our pursuit of Christian
love, and purity of heart. What is more, it is easy to see that those
of us living in the world have nearly endless opportunities for this
kind of co-suffering. Saturated by sexual images in the media, surrounded by indignant and angry people, and utterly assailed with
every kind of commercialist materialism one can imagine, pictures
of sin make up every detail of life in modern society. What is
more, the desperation and suffering caused by all this sin should be
as easy for us to see as it was for Abba Apollos when he saw the face
of the young monk. It is there in the agonized eyes of the homeless
alcoholic, but just as much in the feeble boastings of the wealthy
braggart. It is there in the absent stare of a man entertaining his
lust, and in the empty arrogance of the woman inviting his gaze.
What is more, it is there in our own eyes when we look in the
mirror, complicit as we are in it all.

---

[24] *Conf.* 11.IX.2.

Yet, we must ask how we react to all this sin. Do we abhor it
and cover our eyes? Perhaps at times, and this may not always be the
worst course if we are still deep in the struggle against a particular
passion ourselves. Do we sit in judgment of it? Certainly, though
we should never do so. Or do we, like Abba Apollos, turn our
hearts to the people whose sin we see so clearly, and accept within
ourselves the burden of what they suffer? Do we look at them with
genuine compassion, as though we are looking in a mirror at our
own sins, and say to ourselves "yes, and this is my own transgres-
sion too"? Are we an alcoholic among alcoholics, even though we
seldom drink? Are we a prostitute among prostitutes even though
we are faithful to our spouse? Do we see that our pride is the same
pride as the disdainful boasters on the television screen—or do we
think ourselves a different kind of creature from all these?

It is helpful to observe that repentance through compassion
is perhaps nowhere more available to us than in our mediated relationships with society. Living in the world, we are surrounded
constantly by stories of awful vice and sin, found in the news,
on the web, told through friends and the like. Our usual instinct,
which is one strongly encouraged in the secular world, is to sit
in judgment of the wrongs we hear about on a daily basis, and
probably to grow angry in a way that we perceive to be righteous.
Yet, compassion invites a completely different approach. When
surrounded by real sin and vice, we are welcomed to embrace it
all as our own. Reading a news story on corporate embezzlement,
we are invited to turn to God in earnest and ask forgiveness for
the crime of theft. Hearing about a political sex scandal, we are
encouraged to turn and beg for mercy in the face of our own lust.
Indeed, reading even about the horrors of a murder, we face an
opportunity to ask God to forgive us for taking the lives of his
beloved creatures. If we are not the real perpetrators of such acts,
then it is indeed true that we do not bear the guilt for them, and
will not answer at the judgment as though we do. Yet, if we exercise
compassion, they offer us an even more beautiful chance to turn to
God here and now than our own sins do.

It is easy for most of us to identify at least some of the sinfulness we see around us, and it is easy to see the incredible spiritual danger that exists for anyone living in a society not just rife with, but often fueled by temptation. It is far more difficult to see the simultaneous opportunity that is presented to us by living constantly among those who are tempted, and indeed give in every day to such temptation. Yet, this opportunity is real, and even more present to us than it was to a desert monk like Abba Apollos. Life in society is a string of moments inviting compassion. To seize even one or two of these moments a day would effect a spiritual transformation in us that we could scarcely imagine. It would be to instantly lighten the burden of all those we meet while providing ourselves with one of the greatest blessings we can receive. It would be to heal and be healed in a single act, to repent without needing to be struck first by guilt, to press ourselves and everyone around us forward from anger and into love, which is purity of heart shared in common.

It is certainly the case, however, that most of us will probably spend the vast majority of our time like the foolish elder. If we are not simply complicit in the sin around us (as we usually are), we are most often sitting in judgment of those who are so engaged. Our own failure in this regard, however, can become, once again, an opportunity. As Abba Chaeremon notes, a lack of compassion within us is a sign of how far we still need to go in our struggles.

> Moreover, when a soul has not yet been rendered free of faults, one clear sign is that it does not experience a feeling of mercy in the face of other people's transgressions, but rather clings to rigid, juridical scorn. Indeed, how will it ever be possible for someone to obtain perfection of the heart if he does not have the very thing that can fulfill the whole of the law, as the apostle shows saying, "bear on another's burdens and so fulfill the law of Christ" [Gal 6.2].[25]

For Abba Chaeremon, the degree to which a person is able to exhibit compassion is like a litmus test of the state of her own soul.

[25] *Conf.* II.X.I.

Holy people will always co-suffer with those around them, while, ironically, those who are still in their own sins will sit in judgment.

Therefore, as with charity, there is a negative opportunity in society if we are able to exercise discretion by at least seeing our own lack of compassion. When we fail to take up spiritual co-suffering with another, this failure itself is a sign that there remain within us the marks of our own unrepentance and sin. It shows us that we continue to push ourselves and those around us in the direction of anger, rather than love, and thus participate in preventing our connections to others in society from becoming Christian friendships.

In light of this, we are invited by the *Conferences* to look out upon society and ask what kinds of thoughts and feelings are brought up within us when we see the sins of others. If we are not able to turn our engagement with society into a constant series of experiences of co-suffering compassion, then at the very least we must be able to exercise discretion to turn life in the world into a series of reminders to ourselves of how far we still have to go toward purity of heart. In the world, even more than in the desert, we are invited to turn to compassion and reminded of what it means when we fail to do so.

Patience

So far in this chapter, we have not made much mention of perhaps the greatest Christian virtue that society can help us to cultivate, namely, patience. The term is certainly familiar, but we need to define it precisely if we are going to understand the *Conferences'* teachings.

We begin by observing that patience is something that is developed in our interactions with those who mistreat us. Any time we are wronged, we are given a choice between patience and anger. Such opportunities are like the negative image of our chances to perform charity and good works, arising when *we* find ourselves in need, physical, emotional, or otherwise, and those around us fail to offer help, or perhaps even make the situation worse. Certainly there is no shortage of these experiences for most of us, offered by strangers and colleagues, friends and relatives. What is more, in the world of society, mistreatment and injustice go far beyond our direct relationships. From angry rants in the media or on the web, to severe economic injustices, to anonymous crimes, to corporate heartlessness, most of us spend much of the day being subtly mistreated in one way or another in our mediated relationships as well as our direct ones. The most typical response to injustice and mistreatment in our culture is outrage and resentment. Yet, consistent with the teachings of Abba Joseph on anger, the fathers of the *Conferences* teach that Christians should face mistreatment with a very different attitude. They teach that Christians must seize the opportunity of their own mistreatment by exercising patience.

What, then, is patience exactly? According to Abba Piamun, in the eighteenth conference, patience first reflects an inner humility leading to a gentle endurance of mistreatments.

> Consequently, true humility of heart must be preserved—the kind that does not come from pretenses (either bodily or spoken) but from a deep humility of the mind. This will shine forth by clear evidence (that being patience) when a person … tolerates wrongs done to him, keeping a spirit of goodwill.[26]

The notion that patience involves humbly setting aside concern for ourselves and enduring mistreatment is probably fairly natural to most of us. To the degree that our culture has any sense at all of what patience means, this is it. Yet, real Christian patience means more than just taking whatever another person dishes out. It is related not just to what we endure, but to our inner state while we endure it. Real patience means responding to the anger of another with its natural antidote, namely, love.

The finest illustration in the *Conferences* of this fact about patience comes by way of one of the most vivid stories from the text. Abba Piamun relates the tale of a pious woman who requested from her bishop (St Athanasius, it so happens) that a widow be sent to live with her. In the ancient world, widows were seen as particularly

---

[26]   *Conf.* 18.XI.5.

needy people since they had no husband to provide for them, and often few other options for making a living. Caring for widows was one of the Church's most important missions. The pious woman was thus asking to take on a crucial charitable task. Happy to see such an impulse in a member of his flock, St Athanasius attempted to reward the woman by sending a very generous and kind widow, one who helped around the house and generally made life easier and more pleasant. Yet, the bishop's generosity was met with frustration by the pious woman. She responded back to Athanasius complaining that the widow was too little a burden, and so the bishop had another widow sent to her, this time the most bitter and intolerable that could be found. Abba Piamun explains why.

> She had asked for [a widow] from the bishop not for her refreshment but rather for her torment and annoyance, and, further, in order to carry her over from rest into labor, not labor into rest. So, when the mistreatment [on the part of the second, angry widow] got to the point that she did not hold herself back from lifting a hand to the woman, the other only doubled her works of humble service, and learned to subdue the difficult woman ... with humility.[27]

After a time, the pious woman sent thanks to Bishop Athanasius for sending her an excellent instructor in the art of patience.[28]

This story illustrates something important about patience as Abba Piamun understands it. Where it would have been easy for the pious woman to complain to St Athanasius that her kind gesture had been received with total ingratitude, she saw this ingratitude instead as a chance to develop love. When the widow threw insults at her, she merely increased in ministrations. When the widow tried to hit her, she tended to her all the more. In short, as the widow ramped up her anger, moving in the wrong direction away from the pole of love, the pious woman ramped up her love, moving away from the pole of anger. Patience is precisely this—to respond to

27   *Conf.* 18.XIV.4.
28   *Conf.* 18.XIV.5.

whatever degree of anger we face with Christian love to the same degree.

To exercise patience so defined has at least one, and usually two, profound effects on human beings. To begin with, the patient person naturally grows in love by actually using the mistreatment of the world as a spur to that love. Life in society provides no shortage of mistreatment and anger directed at us. If, through patience, this anger pushes us to love all the more, then we will find ourselves growing in love on an exponential curve, grateful, as was the pious woman, for the insults of other people that now push us in this direction. Second, patience often allows us to live out the teachings of Abba Joseph regarding our responsibility for the anger of others. According to the story, the pious woman slowly assuaged the widow's anger by continuing to perform good works of charity toward her. Unrelenting in her patience, the pious woman took responsibility for the widow's anger, and so eventually began to dissolve it. Our patience is not always met by other people eventually coming to love us more, but it often is. Like compassion, it is a tool of interpersonal healing that, by extension, is therefore a tool of growth in mutual purity of heart.

It is important to be clear that we as Christians do not excuse or accept mistreatment when we exercise patience. Quite the contrary, patience *requires* that we see mistreatment for what it is. The angry widow's treatment of the pious woman was a violation of the latter's humanity—a totally unacceptable reaction from the Christian point of view, and the pious woman made no claim whatsoever to the contrary. Had the pious woman excused the widow's behavior, and pretended that the latter had done nothing wrong, she could not have used the widow's mistreatment as a spur toward love. We as Christians must therefore exercise discernment to see situations of mistreatment for what they are.

Recognizing this matters a lot in our world, in part because we must be clear that those who find themselves in situations of truly severe abuse should by no means assume that they ought merely to tolerate their treatment, or try to emulate the pious woman in an

outward way. Her exterior behavior is appropriate for us in the face
of the mundane forms of mistreatment that we all experience on a
daily basis—frustrated words from a stranger, an arrogant boss at
work, a hateful celebrity on TV, perhaps a grumpy or even angry
spouse. But, patience does not require us as Christians to remain
present in a severely abusive relationship, a situation of domestic
violence, or anything of the sort. Quite the contrary, to do so
would be inconsistent with the teachings of the fathers. Precisely
because we are responsible for the anger of other people, it is critical to discern when the best thing we can do for them, as well as
ourselves, is to remove ourselves from their presence either permanently or temporarily. Should the reader find himself in a situation
of serious abuse, he should seek out help, probably beginning with
his parish priest, to begin the work of discerning what patient love
really requires of him, with all options very much on the table.

Let us turn our minds back, however, to the more everyday
kinds of mistreatment that are the real topic of the widow's story.
We are becoming accustomed in our discussion to thinking not
just about virtue in the Christian life, but also about what it means
for us when virtue is absent. In the case of patience, a failure to
manifest virtue typically comes in one of two forms. First, we fail
in patience whenever we find ourselves openly expressing our anger.
We may simply mutter something in irritation, make a rude gesture, shout at another person in rage, or even go so far as to start
throwing fists. We have access to myriad expressions of anger, and
when we notice ourselves engaging in them, then we have a sure
sign that we are not cultivating patience. We have already seen that
Abba Joseph teaches that Christians must make sure to hold their
tongue in the event that they grow angry with another person.[29]
This is because escalating a situation by making our anger openly
manifest almost never helps in the work of guiding ourselves and
others toward love. Outwardly restraining ourselves is therefore a
small but important first step toward real patience. Yet, bold-faced

---

[29] See p. 60. See p. 60.

angry reactions are far from the only way that we can manifest a break-down in patience. Far more common, perhaps for Christians especially, is false humility.

False humility, according to the *Conferences*, involves our pretending to be patient outwardly while silently harboring anger within ourselves. Abba Piamun teaches that if we put on the face of false humility in response to mistreatment, we invite spiritual pride and deepen the anger between ourselves and others.[30] For one thing, false humility very often turns back into overt anger eventually, albeit often in subtle ways. We may put up with an irritation for a time, but then we eventually declare that we have had enough and "stand up for ourselves" by throwing mistreatment right back at our enemy. Or, we may stew about our problem in silent self-righteousness and refuse to speak to the other person. Or, we may feign our humility to the extreme, allowing ourselves to engage in the sin of self-loathing in an unconscious hope that, by our heaping suffering upon ourselves, everyone around us will begin to consider us a victim, and then turn on our enemy. In every such case, false humility leads to our taking action that drives a wedge between ourselves and other people, and encourages us, and others, to race away from love and toward anger.

What is more, even if we really do manage to avoid all outward works of anger, including the subtle types, so long as we silently harbor anger toward another by way of false humility, patience remains impossible. It is easy to see why. If, in our inner selves, we pursue the pole of anger in response to another person, then no matter what we do outwardly we are, by definition, failing to react to mistreatment wholly with love, and such a loving reaction is the very definition of patience. Indeed, in accordance with the teachings of Abba Joseph, where anger is, patience cannot be.

A state of false humility can be particularly difficult to disentangle, especially in our world. Much of society today has become so divorced from images of real patience that false humility is

---

[30] *Conf.* 18.XI.1–5.

earnestly mistaken for the genuine article. This can cause us entirely to forget to attend to our inner anger, and, in so doing,
deepen our sin and that of others. We can also fall into the trap of
thinking that our choice not to express our anger, since it really is
the right choice for the Christian in most cases, is a good enough
step toward love, and that we can rest content after having held our
tongue without looking to cleanse our inner person. Yet, we have
already clearly seen that the fathers teach that this inner cleansing
is not only important, but is the *most* important step toward developing patience and thereby Christian love.

The antidote for false humility is discretion. Indeed, the
hopeful news about all our failures to exercise patience is that, in
accordance with Abba Piamun, such failures—whether manifest as
open anger or false humility—can themselves become an opportunity to see a lack of virtue in ourselves and thus to begin to address
that lack. He teaches that acts of impatience and anger all reflect a
"hidden weakness" within us.[31] This small observation leads us to
notice that when we see ourselves acting without patience, we are
given a chance, through discretion, to see also the inner weakness
that it reflects. When we see ourselves angry inwardly or outwardly,
we must turn to consider our own lack of patience and so begin to
turn back to patience once again.

In light of the problem of false humility, this means that we
must take extreme care to monitor our responses to other people,
especially our inward reactions, in order to see where they lead us.
While false humility and a lack of patience inevitably give way to
anger and resentment in the long run,[32] real patience and humility
eventually bloom into peace, tranquility, joy and especially love,
even if mistreatment continues. If, through discretion, we observe
the emotional, psychological, and material fruits of the inner state

---

[31]   *Conf.* 18.XIII.3.
[32]   See the story in *Conf.* 18.XI.1–4 of a monk who continually feigned humility
in the face of kindness from other monks, only to collapse into anger at the
tiniest criticism.

that we cultivate in the face of mistreatment, we can begin the process of cultivating real patience in ourselves.

For lay Christians, this work of monitoring the self and taking note of anger will occupy much more of our time than the exercise of real and genuine patience. While the pious woman's attitude must remain our ideal, we must be very careful not to make the mistake of aping her in an outward sense before we have established something of her inner character (in other words, the mistake of false humility). A life in which we seek to cultivate patience in society is far more likely to include a constant cycling back to our own lack thereof than it is to be constituted by a series of patient acts. Yet, this cycling back can lead us to the real patience we seek, and so our experience of society ever remains a tool for seeking purity of heart when through discretion we are honest about our inner state.

We should make a special note here about mediated relationships. We call our attention to such relationships because they are particularly good sites for the work of developing patience. While our social instincts tend to push us to be at least fairly cordial most of the time to people who are actually in the same room with us, such instincts seem not to kick in as often when we engage in mediated relationships of various sorts. In mediated relationships, we find ourselves capable of thinking and speaking vitriol that we would never dream of voicing to someone in person. Perhaps that involves swearing loudly at the people on TV, or insulting an interlocutor on a web forum, or cursing a politician we particularly dislike—whatever the mediated relationship, the problem is the same. On the other side of the coin, mediated relationships are also often the site of more acute and biting forms of mistreatment than we tend to receive in personal encounters. We may well be on the receiving end of the same kind of unchecked rancor we so often dish out. Yet, precisely because of these facts, mediated relationships offer us a particularly clear opportunity for the development of patience. Since we tend to find ourselves escalating far more quickly in the context of mediated relationships than we do with personal ones, it is often substantially easier to see whether our encounters with others are being driven by love or by anger. Mediation strips away most of the social niceties that can cover over the emotional reactions that, according to the fathers, are the fruits of the inner self. It thus, ironically, assuages the problem of false humility to some extent by exacerbating our straightforward anger. Mediated relationships can therefore be excellent tools for the exercise of discretion. If we are angry over politics, bitter over a bad job market, frustrated by a lack of acknowledgement at work, then we have clear proof that we have not yet fully developed patience, else it would manifest in every case.

The world, then, is a place where we can make immense progress in cultivating patience, which means meeting the anger of others with equal portions of love. Because we are so often mistreated, and in so many ways, if we turn every instance of our own mistreatment into a spur of love, we will find society not merely less of an impediment in our pursuit of purity of heart, but one of our greatest resources.

The Kingdom through the World

In many ways, society is simply people, and this is why we have been focusing on relationships in this chapter. For us, people in society must become sites of genuine love.

Yet, we have left off one last observation about what Christian love really means. While it is a commonplace today to think of love as a precious ideal, it is critical to recall, as we have already noted, that the fathers of the *Conferences* did not see love as merely an outpouring of positive emotion, or some strong connection of fondness. As we have said, real love, for them, is a total mutual commitment to purity of heart. This has profound implications. As we have seen, when we attain our Christian goal of purity of heart, we also begin to realize our *telos*, the kingdom of God. This is true with respect to Christian love as well, since realizing such love means realizing mutual purity of heart. Thus, when real love is present, the *telos* of that love is present as well.

What is this *telos* in the case of loving relationships? Nothing short of God. Indeed, for the fathers, love *is* God in an absolute sense, and thus, when love is present in a relationship, God is literally there as well.

> Finally, so highly is the virtue of love extolled that the blessed Apostle John declares that it not only belongs to God, but that it *is* God, saying: "God is love: he, therefore, that abides in love, abides in God, and God in him" [I Jn 4.16]. For so far do we see that love is divine, that we find that what the apostle says is plainly a living truth in us: "For the love of God is poured into our hearts by the Holy Spirit who dwells in us" [Rom 5.5]. He could equally have said that God is poured into our hearts by the Holy Spirit who dwells in us.[33]

The fathers take St John's famous statement that "God is love" absolutely literally. Let us be clear about what this means for us. When charity, compassion, and patience are manifest in our relationships, love begins to bloom. And when love is present God is literally present there, manifest as love within us. This is the reason that it is critical to see that all good works, as important as they are in the Christian life, remain secondary kinds of good. For, according to Abba Moses, love, unlike good works of charity, compassion, and even patience, remains with us even in the kingdom of God. It does not pass away, like these other works, when man's fallen nature is dismissed.

> For all useful and necessary gifts are granted for a while, and then, at the completion of the allotted time, they of course quickly pass away. Love, though—love is never stolen off. For not only does it work steadfastly in us in the present age, but it will also endure in the one to come (though the burden of bodily needs will be gone)—it will endure and become even more efficacious and wonderful.[34]

---

[33] *Conf.* 16.XIII.1. Translation adapted from Gibson.
[34] *Conf.* 1.XI.2.

For the fathers, God is love, and love remains with the human creature even in the kingdom of God, even growing there, in fact. Love,
then, is an earnest of the kingdom of God itself. Like *theoria*, genuine love is an experience of our real *telos* to which we have access
right here in this life. To transform our relationships with others
into sites of love is to experience already in the present world a
taste of the kingdom.

Our life in society, then, is meant to be a life lived in a series
of relationships each of which bear within them the kingdom of
God. If each of our relationships were to be what it should, then
the kingdom would be everywhere around us all the time. If we
imagine for a moment what it might be like to realize an experience
of the kingdom every time we so much as think of another person,
then we can see quite clearly how lofty and holy a call we who live
in society have received. Such a meditation on the intended *telos* of
our lives in society ought to drive us with profound force toward
the charity, compassion, and patience that can help us to realize the
love that makes it possible.

Yet, society remains a deeply broken place. We, and those
around us, stand in the way of what could come to exist between
all human beings. We do this through anger in all its forms. The
fathers of the *Conferences,* however, do not look upon this situation
with despair. To them, as we have seen throughout this chapter, our
social vices are as much an opportunity to begin building love as
are our moments of virtue. When we experience anger, judgment,
false humility, and the like, they reflect something back to us about
ourselves. The company of other human beings, *especially* in broken
relationships, must therefore become a window onto ourselves.
When we pass by a beggar, we must see that we have passed by the
presence of God. When we become angry, we must see that as high
as our anger rises, so deep could our love be if we were to set anger
aside. When we judge another, we must see that his sins are our
own. When we falsify humility, we must see that our real patience
can be all that our forgery only feigns to become.

In light of all this, it is no surprise that in the nineteenth conference, Abba John teaches that human society can and must be a
tool for Christian salvation. So important a tool is society, in fact,
that he teaches that desert hermits must actually make up for their
absence from society by imagining the kinds of experiences that
they would have had there.

> Thus, human interaction is not only no impediment to reme-
> dying the vices that we have discussed so far, but it confers a lot
> of benefit. For the more often the incidents of their impatience
> are exposed (and thus the greater is the lingering pain of those
> oppressed by them), the more quickly do others produce health
> in those working toward it. As such, even while remaining in sol-
> itude—where the causes and substance of irritation cannot spill
> out from other people—we must deliberately trot out [mental]
> incitements thereto.[35]

As we live in the world, angered by politicians, judgmental of those
we meet, faking humility and holiness—as we live in the world
mistreated by our friends, our coworkers, strangers, governments
and economies, newspaper columnists and TV personalities—as
we live in the broken world, breaking it yet further and feeling
the pain of its fallenness, we must recall the teachings of the fathers that are summarized here by Abba John. At every moment,
of highest joy and deepest pain, society can and must be a tool for
our salvation and a place wherein we touch the kingdom of God.

---

[35] *Conf.* 19.XVI.1–2.

Chapter 3

Marriage and Family

How very good and pleasant it is when kindred live together in unity!
Psalm 132.1 (LXX)

At the moment when a couple is crowned and thus martyred to one another, a new Orthodox family begins. By God's grace, we pray that these new families eventually grow to include children, whether natural or adopted, and so begin the work of handing the gospel down to a new generation for its preservation and preaching. In many ways, a wedding is to life in the world what a tonsuring is to the life of a monk. It finalizes a decision and celebrates a call to a particular way of seeking the kingdom of God. By the same token, a family, for the lay person, serves much the same role in Christian life as a monastery serves for monks and nuns. While we live much of our lives away from it, it is inevitably to our home and family that we return as a center and spiritual focal point. A family is an entity of its own—a coherent organism with its own character and qualities. Yet, a family, like society as we explored it in the previous chapter, is also a web of relationships. Most central of these is the married relationship between husband and wife, which relationship ideally matures over time to include children just as a tree with one trunk eventually grows many branches.

Because a family constitutes a group of relationships, the basic means by which we can make it a tool for obtaining purity of heart are founded on the essential understanding of relationships that we outlined in the previous chapter. There we discussed the teachings of Abba Joseph on friendship, the ideal Christian relationship, in which both parties strive in absolute virtue toward purity of heart and thus develop genuine love. Christian family relationships are not different with regard to their ideal form. They, like all relationships, are meant to become Christian friendships built on genuine love. To this end, it is important to note that many of the practices critical for developing love that we identified in the previous chapter are just as applicable to family relationships as to life in society. Indeed, any married couple knows the power of simple acts of kindness and charity within a marriage to heal wounds and nourish love. Any father knows how much easier it is to love his child when he takes a moment to enter into that child's experience through genuine compassion and co-suffering. And any mother knows the critical importance of patience in a family, for the lofty ideal of Abba Joseph is most often not a manifest reality in the home any more than it is in the city.

We have already said much, however, about these concepts. In this chapter, we will build on this foundation and examine some of the unique aspects of the work of cultivating this kind of love in family relationships specifically. In the first section, we will discuss the importance of developing a unity of purpose in a Christian family if love is to become possible there. In the second section, we will examine how the protective instinct helps nurture real love in Christian families. In the third section, we will discuss married sexuality in light of the *Conferences.* In the fourth and final section, we will approach several of the most difficult passages in the *Conferences*—difficult, that is, in that they are easy to misunderstand from the point of view of a married reader.

The Goal of Family Life: Unity of Purpose

In this section we will discuss the importance in family life of developing unity of purpose, a concept we will define in a moment. We will begin by examining the married relationship, and will move on to discuss unity of purpose in the parent-child relationship a little later on.

According to Abba Joseph, in order to cultivate genuine love, any relationship must be constructed on a foundational unity of purpose.

> And therefore, love can carry on undisturbed in those who maintain one commitment and one intention with each other—willing the same thing, willing against the same thing. If you, also, want to keep such a love protected, you must be quick first to kill your own will by expelling the vices, and next to fulfill eagerly that in which the prophet so greatly delights: "behold how good and joyful a thing it is for brethren to dwell together in unity" [Ps 133.1].[1]

For Abba Joseph, unity of purpose means the maintaining of a single will between two people. It is accomplished when individuals strive toward one, unified goal. As we have already seen clearly, for Christians that goal, according to the *Conferences*, is shared purity of heart. Indeed, it could almost go without saying that it is only in a relationship in which both individuals strive for the one goal of purity of heart that real love (which is simply shared purity of heart) can ever exist. Just as Abba Joseph says, then, unity of purpose is prerequisite to love.

For this reason, according to Abba Joseph, all Christian relationships require unity of purpose. However, in the context of marriage, the need for unity of purpose is especially pronounced. Most couples probably have a sense already that a division of wills and desires within a marriage will spell trouble at least, if not eventual disaster, as the couple tries to navigate the many decisions that they must make throughout their lives together. When two people pull in fundamentally different directions, real and deep conflict becomes not only possible but inevitable. A wife who desires nothing but money, for example, and a husband who feels called to become a priest, are quite likely to battle one another tooth and nail as they make decisions both big and small. Without a unity of will, and a single orientation to purity of heart, a marriage

---

[1]   *Conf.* 16.III.4.

becomes a power struggle, and eventually a battle ground, as each party attempts to jockey its way to control and thereby to guide the marriage to the pursuit of this or that preferred end. When this begins to happen, the couple will inevitably drift apart, as they so often do in the modern world, and even if they remain married, they will live increasingly as strangers under a single roof. As Abba Joseph again notes, "at no time can peace be kept whole where a disagreement of wills arises."[2] The common sense of this teaching ought to be evident to anyone.

If, however, the need for unity of purpose is especially pronounced in marriage, the possibility of attaining it is also much greater than in most of our relationships. Married couples simply spend far more time together and make far more decisions together than people do in other relationships. As such, marriage offers daily opportunities to hone the work of uniting purpose and will. If these are seized, then unity of purpose can develop more rapidly in a marriage than in any other relationship. Yet, we cannot say much more before we know how unity of purpose is established according to the *Conferences*. Let us attend to this question now.

After saying in the above quotation that love can only exist in a relationship built on a unity of purpose, Abba Joseph identifies two key steps that must be taken by individuals in order to develop it. First, they must overcome their own vices. This idea is quite natural in light of what we have said about Christian love. Two people will not draw closer to their goal of purity of heart if each of them clings to their own private barriers to that purity. In order to grow in their goal together, they must, by definition, grow in it individually. Those seeking purity of heart in their marriage, then, must begin by turning within and initiating the work of eradicating vice and promoting virtue within themselves. If two people in a marriage both take this step, then a great deal has already been accomplished, and the rich soil required to cultivate purity of heart has been spread within their relationship.

---

[2]   *Conf.* 16.III.5.

The second step to unity that Abba Joseph identifies requires somewhat more comment. He says that people must surrender their will to one another if they are to share the same goal. The surrendering of one's will to his or her spouse in this way is, in essence, an act of humility. We defined humility in chapter one as the work of letting go one's own desires and judgments in favor of those of another, and ultimately of God.

There may be much, however, that is difficult for many of us living in contemporary society to grasp about married humility. It can be hard for us to conceive that the handing over of the will to another person that Abba Joseph describes above has nothing to do with power, control, or even basic decision making in a household. Humility, in this and any context, does not amount to the act of one human will simply submitting to the power of whatever another human will desires as though this submission itself is the point. Real humility, instead, amounts to the submitting of the human will to the will of God, with the will of other people acting as intermediary. Humility in a marriage, then, does not amount to wife or husband simply responding with "yes dear" to whatever the other desires. It involves, instead, the submission of the human will of both parties to the will of God *by way of* submission first to one another.

How is this possible? To answer this question, we must first reiterate that before the humble submission of the will to another in a Christian friendship, Abba Joseph assumes that both parties have committed themselves to the pursuit of purity of heart alone. It is the fact that real married humility is preceded by a commitment to the pursuit of purity of heart that makes it possible for the submitting of two wills to one another to transform into the submission of both wills to God. When both parties seek purity of heart in a marriage, the vicissitudes of each person's individual desires do not alter the direction of the relationship, no matter what specific obstacles or opportunities arise. Whether the husband makes a particular choice, or the wife, each seeks to choose that which cultivates purity of heart, and so they are united in every decision, even if they never discuss it before hand. What is more, because both parties direct themselves to the same place, they are each guided by the other to this goal in a feedback loop of sorts wherein neither husband nor wife fundamentally leads, but both direct one another at once. What occurs within a marriage built on humility of this sort is often difficult to describe or even understand. Over time, the marriage ceases to be controlled by one person or the other, and begins to be controlled by something much larger than either husband or wife alone—something that they likely cannot quite put a finger on, but that seems to guide their steps as they walk with one another.

In accordance with the teachings of Abba Joseph, this something is genuine love. Abba Joseph is clear in indicating that when two people really do cultivate purity of heart, and then humble themselves to one another, thus attaining unity of purpose, love becomes manifest in them. This kind of love is not something we are accustomed to thinking about in the context of marriage. It does not resemble the romantic passion or even the strong sense of fondness that is so often celebrated in our culture. Instead, this love is a veritable and palpable force—almost approaching a phys-ical presence—that begins to exist in the ever-diminishing space between husband and wife as they grow to become true Christian friends. It is a love that has a will and a sense of purpose, a direc-tionality and a sweeping power that draws two people forward as if flowing in the currents of an unseen river toward the kingdom of God. When unity of purpose is established in a marriage, the love that it cultivates becomes a thinking thing, a conscious being with its own will.

This way of experiencing Christian love in a marriage devoted to unity of purpose should come as no surprise given the teach-ings of the *Conferences*. For, as we have noted in the conclusion to chapter two, such genuine love quite literally *is* God, present within the relationship that has invited him by being directed toward purity of heart alone. In this sense, the married couple who have cultivated mutual purity of heart and humbled themselves to one another become, very literally, a vessel of the kingdom of God—a site of the kingdom's real presence in the world. The will that becomes manifest in their love is the very will of God. The force of love that sweeps them forward is God himself. It is so that their individual wills become wholly unnecessary and superfluous, and that their humble submission to one another becomes not a submission to any human being, but to God. The wills of husband and wife can thus "die," as Abba Joseph puts it,[3] ultimately ceasing to be, while the relationship itself drives forward, navigating every challenge from the simplest of decisions about the dinner menu, to the greatest of life's conundrums, doing so more easily than could previously have been dreamed.

Such are the profound implications of Abba Joseph's teaching on unity of purpose for married couples. These same teachings, however, also have serious implications for our understanding of what the relationship between parents and children must become in a Christian family. While there are myriad images of what an ideal parent-child relationship should look like in today's world, basically none of them resemble in any way a Christian friendship based on purity of heart, humility and absolute unity in striving for the kingdom of God. Far more often, even among many Christians, children are presented as creations of their parents, virtual non-entities whose character, beliefs, conduct, and future are dictated entirely by those who raise them. They are seen as lumps of clay to be molded in this way or that for the purpose of building a particular kind of person who will be able to succeed according to a given set of criteria (sometimes including religious criteria) that happens to be valued by parent and community. The basic understanding is that parents control this process of molding, and success is defined by the degree to which the eventual adult product meets a particular standard of what is desirable. Parental choices are, in turn, judged (often quite openly and rudely) on the quality

---

[3]   *Conf.* 16.III.4. Quoted above on p. 93.

of the product that they produce in the same way that a craftsman's technique is judged by his work.

Abba Joseph's teaching on unity of purpose, however, demands that Orthodox Christians approach the work of parenting in a completely different way. The goal of Christian parenting must become not the molding of a particular kind of successful adult product, but the development of a true Christian friendship between parent and child—one that is built on genuine love that is shared purity of heart. Such a friendship, it nearly goes without saying, will not resemble what is commonly called "friendship" in secular society. It will not be a relationship of two social peers, for children are not peers of their parents in age, knowledge, or wisdom. Parents and children will not become buddies, mom and dad will not be perceived as cool and with-it most of the time. The friendship between parent and child will remain imbalanced in regards to knowledge, and until those children become adults themselves, also in regards to power over decision making. Yet, the Christian parent-child relationship, if it is to live up to the ideal presented by Abba Joseph, will always and necessarily be a nascent and growing Christian friendship, and thus it will always be a relationship between two *people*.

What is so often forgotten in popular culture is this simple fact: that children are people. Those seeking to apply the teachings of the *Conferences* in their family lives will have to begin by understanding that their children are real human beings of their own. A human relationship cannot and does not exist between the sculptor and his clay, or between the cabinet-maker and his furniture. Real relationships of love exist only between genuine human agents, even if a differential of wisdom and power are necessarily present. More to the point here, unity of purpose is accomplished not when one of these human agents outwardly resembles the other in some particular capacity, nor is it achieved when a child lives up to the expectations of a parent. Conversely, it is not precluded when a child falls short of a parent's worldly ideal, nor is it made impossible when he or she fails to meet the expectations of a particular worldly community. No, unity of purpose is achieved when two people strive together for purity of heart in humility, and thus make the kingdom of God literally manifest within themselves.

The first step to take in order to develop unity of purpose with our children, then, is to practice the virtues and thus cultivate purity of heart ourselves. This is the necessary starting point in all our relationships according to Abba Joseph, but when it comes to children it is doubly important. This is because children naturally emulate their parents when they are young, and often begin to do so again when they start to become adults (and, in fact, even while they are teenagers, they emulate their parents at least a little, if often secretly). Thus, as we cultivate purity of heart and take the first step toward unity of purpose with our children, we are accomplishing much the same cultivation within our children as well, and thereby guiding them to the same first step. We stand as in an echo chamber where what we nurture in ourselves is nurtured in our children.

When it comes to children, however, the second step that Abba Joseph teaches we must take toward unity of purpose—the development of humility—is substantially more tricky to understand. While we quite rightly expect that our children will defer themselves to our will, it is much more difficult for us to accept that we must defer ourselves to them. Perhaps the biggest reason for this is that parents cannot (and should not) defer themselves to their children with regard to simple basic desires. This is because even a child who has developed a sense of the importance of purity of heart will nonetheless know very little about how to actually develop it. She cannot, even if she wants to, be a full partner in the work of setting aside the vices and pursuing the one goal of all Christians whole-heartedly. She must be taught how to do this, and in the process of this teaching, parents must exercise substantial authority. The exercise of authority may seem, at first blush, to preclude the exercise of humility. Yet, this need not be the case necessarily.

The central means by which we can develop humility while exercising parental authority is by practicing discretion in relation to our responses to our children. Because we cannot count on our children to know the best ways to set aside their vices and seek love, we must replace this knowledge on their part with our own understanding of what love requires. This work of replacement is accomplished if all the decisions we make on their behalf are driven wholly and exclusively by love. We recall that the fullness of humility amounts to the submission of one's will to God, rather than to another person. If we, as parents, take charge of our children's decisions as we must, and in turn ensure that we are motivating these decisions entirely by real Christian love, then we can be comfortable that these same decisions are therefore motivated in turn by God, for, as we have said a few times now, God is love.

When we constantly exercise discretion with regard to the seemingly infinite decisions that we have to make about and for our children, and thus begin to submit ourselves to them in humility, we have a similar experience to that which we explored already in the context of marriage. We begin to realize that what is directing our choices for them is not our own fickle desire. Instead, it is something greater than ourselves as individuals. As in marriage, this love has a will of its own, an orientation of its own, and it draws us and our children along, blooming within our relationship. We find ourselves astounded to be learning something from our children, even the smallest ones, about what it means to be human and what it means to love God, often even feeling that we have learned much more than we have taught. We find our hearts warmed to see them emulating our best qualities, and are reminded of how far we need to go when we see them emulating our worst ones. We surprise ourselves with what we permit, what we deny. We find ourselves forgiving effortlessly, and far more striking, we find ourselves asking forgiveness even from a child too small to speak. We thus see God's will guiding us and our children as we submit ourselves to it in humility.

Our children, in turn, quite often begin ever more easily to submit their wills in obedience to us as parents, and thereby to God, when we practice humility this way. When our decisions are scrutinized in discretion, and thus turned over to the direction of love, our children's natural inclination to experiment with disobedience is remarkably assuaged (though probably not eliminated). If we have succeeded in helping them to desire purity of heart first, and we, too, direct ourselves to the will of the God who is love, then our children most often see and gravitate toward our will as it becomes ever clearer to them that by way of their submission to us, love grows more manifest in ourselves and our home. It is, after all, much easier to do as a parent says when one knows for certain that in so doing love will grow. In short, when we and our children submit to one another by first directing ourselves to the love that is shared purity of heart, then, despite the parental responsibility to exercise power and make decisions, real humility and thus unity of purpose is indeed possible between parent and child.

Many volumes could be (and are being) written about Orthodox parenting. Here, we do not speak anywhere near exhaustively on the topic. Instead, we have looked only to discuss whether and how developing unity of purpose, and the humility it requires, can be accomplished in a parent-child relationship. Dozens of important topics from discipline, to education, to prayer in the home must be left aside. What is more, if our discussion thus far makes it sound like Christian parenting is easy, this is only because of the brevity of time which we have devoted to the topic. As with all things in life, developing unity of purpose with our children is a messy and difficult process. This is not least because establishing the virtue of discretion in oneself is a profoundly difficult task, and developing unity of purpose with one's children relies heavily on this virtue's presence in the Christian parent.

Yet, we have seen something important. As with marriage, the kingdom of God can become present in our relationships with our children through unity of purpose. Even if we have only managed to call our attention to this simple fact, and point in the direction of how to make it a manifest reality, this remains a critical lesson to take from the *Conferences*. What is more, to see the green shoots of the kingdom beginning to grow between parent and child is one of the most moving experiences a Christian can have. In these moments, we see with clear eyes our love, the kingdom, which has such indescribable power, which moves us to tears at the thought of a little smiling face, present or remembered, which springs forth from the heart when that dearest set of arms is wrapped around our neck in a hug. What is more, we see love reflected back in our children's eyes, realizing only by gazing into those tiny mirrors that it has come alive within us as well, and that they, too, feel the joy of its presence between us. When we see this love, the kingdom, within ourselves and our children, we know that we do not desire for them the success of this world, nor failure, riches, nor poverty, fame, nor anonymity, but rather that we desire only that this love, the kingdom, will grow within them and within us eternally. When we see this love, the kingdom, we know that they, too, desire only that this love will remain with us and between us forever, for we see that our purpose and theirs is one. When we therefore realize that the only desire we have left for our children, and they for us, is the purity of heart that welcomes this kingdom, then we have come to the unity of purpose that Abba Joseph tells us is the beginning of the genuine love that is God himself.

In accordance with the teachings of Abba Joseph, a family united by a single purpose is a family in which the first seeds of love have been planted. The presence of these seeds of love is an absolute prerequisite to a Christian family becoming a tool for seeking the kingdom on the part of all its members. Yet, as with all of our relationships, much more than the recognition of an ideal is needed in a Christian family, and no matter how powerful are those moments in which we see real love, they do not last forever, and do not sustain themselves without effort on our part. Love is difficult to foster, yet, there are a few unique aspects of family life that make it especially possible to cultivate love there. To some of these we turn now.

Protection and Holy Fear

As we have said, in striving for purity of heart and the kingdom of God through unity of purpose, a family presents an opportunity to develop Christian love in precisely the same ways as we develop it within any other set of relationships—through doing good to one another, showing genuine compassion, and humbling ourselves to each other. We have ample opportunities for practicing these virtues within a family. Nowhere else are we more likely to see the needs of another person, so as to provide charity, or to be exposed to the inner workings of their mind and soul so as to suffer along with them, or to find ourselves in a position to exercise patience. If nothing else, then, our simple proximity to the others in our family can and should become an opportunity to exercise even more fully the virtues that are required to turn any relationship into a site for the realization of the kingdom of God.

However, the fathers of the *Conferences* do cast family relationships as spiritually unique, not in the sense that they are meant to become something fundamentally different from other Christian relationships, but because they usually have a distinct advantage over our relationships with other people in our lives. People in families, according to the fathers, are naturally disposed toward treating one another with a particular kind of affection, as Abba Joseph teaches.

> But there is another kind of love, one that is brought about from natural instinct and the rules of blood relationships. With this kind of love, a person's clansmen, spouse, parents, siblings or children are all naturally preferred to anyone else. This is observed not just in the human species, but also with every bird and animal. For they protect and defend their nestlings or their babies by natural instinct, to the point that they are often not afraid to expose themselves to risks—even death—for them.[4]

Abba Joseph goes on to say that the protective instinct is one of the stronger emotional forces that can bind people together. It is

[4]   *Conf.* 16.II.2.

104 A LAYMAN IN THE DESERT

a natural instinct in the most literal sense—it is seen in human beings, but also in animals.

Now, Abba Joseph is quick to note that the protective instinct is still a worldly force, one that does not necessarily last eternally. A bond such as this, Abba Joseph teaches, can break down for all sorts of reasons, even in a family.

> For, often, separation of place interrupts and breaks off [rela-tionships], as does losing touch over time and through silence, along with the goings-on of law-suits or other conflicts. [These relationships] usually come from various connections of profit, desire, family relations, or acquaintance, and, as such, they are let go as soon as some cause for division gets in the way.[5]

This observation on his part ought to be fairly obvious to us in a world in which so many families fall apart so easily, and family re-lationships based on simple fondness and natural instinct descend into dysfunction and estrangement. Whether a family relationship cools because of simple distance and time apart, or is broken down by angry words, emotional discord, or in extreme cases, abuse, there is nothing about the natural protective instinct that makes it necessarily permanent. Indeed, quite possibly the biggest mis-understanding about the nature of family in our modern world is found in the failing to notice, as Abba Joseph does, that the instinctive ties that bind are not enough to hold human beings together in love. It is not uncommon today to encounter people who seem to expect that family members will love one another and carry on loving one another out of sheer natural disposition— because that is what people in families are meant to do. What is worse is that this expectation of natural love can be and often is used as an excuse for neglecting the spiritual needs of our family relationships, as though we assume that they are already so strong as not to require any further assistance. Abba Joseph is quite right, however. Natural instinct within a family is not sufficient grounds on which to develop real Christian love. Instead, as he teaches, real love can only be built when family relationships begin to become true Christian friendships, and foster unity of purpose as we have seen.

Nonetheless, the protective instinct can be extremely helpful in our efforts to develop such Christian friendships within a family. The protective instinct, while it is not the same thing as Christian love, can help to catalyze love in family relationships when that love *is* based on unity of purpose and is therefore a manifestation of the kingdom. This is because the protective instinct helps drive virtuous behavior within families.

To begin with, the protective instinct naturally spurs our desire to do good to one another in charity. When we want to protect someone and see them in need, we are far more likely to help them as we should. It does not take much for a parent to motivate herself to help her child when he is hurt. A loving husband is easily moved to do much more around the house just after a baby is born. Children, especially young children, are profoundly inclined to offer the assistance they can to their parents, however small and marginally helpful it might, in fact, be. These things are made easier (though by no means automatic) in families because of the protective instinct.

What is more, the protective instinct creates a natural inclination to treat one another with compassion. When we hate to see a family member suffering because of our instinctive desire to protect them, this feeling makes it easier to accept their suffering as our own. Parents in particular are likely to understand this impulse to seek to experience a child's pain for themselves, whether that pain results from a simple skinned knee or the far-reaching impact of sin on the world. In the same way, when we see our family members struggling in the vices, we too struggle with those vices almost by definition because of the pain that it causes us to see a spouse or children suffer. In a family, the vices impact everyone in the home quite directly, and the sins of our spouse or children become our own sins whether we consent to them ourselves or not. If we keep the lesson of the foolish elder and the young monk in mind,[6] this experience of being thrust into compassion can and should help to cultivate love within our family relationships. With regard to charity and compassion, then, our protective instinct helps us practice these virtues instinctively and thus far more often.

Yet, far beyond facilitating the key virtues of charity and compassion, the *Conferences* make clear that the protective instinct, when combined with a recognition of Christian love, introduces a powerful force into family life that is difficult to cultivate in any other relationship. This force is holy fear. The word fear may seem surprising here. After all, we hope never to fear anyone in our family in the most common sense of the word. Indeed, fear in the sense of fright is the mark of a totally broken family relationship, a relationship involving abuse, and thus should be the cause of utmost concern. But we mean something different by the words "holy fear"—indeed, something totally the opposite of fright. We mean a fear of hurting one another—a fear of causing offense toward the love that we share in our family. Holy fear is the experience of terror at the thought of losing genuine Christian love, as Abba Chaeremon teaches in the eleventh conference.

> So, whoever has arrived at the perfection of such love will necessarily climb up, one step of excellence at a time, to the sublime fear of love. This fear is not from the dread of punishments, or the desire for rewards. Rather, it is born upon the heights of love. It is that fear by which the son earnestly honors his doting father, a brother his brother, a friend her friend, a husband his wife. For they do not fear blows or insults, but rather they fear any damage being done to their love, and they take diligent care not just in everything they do, but in every word they speak, lest something should make tepid the warmth of the other's love.[7]

The fear of compromising our love for one another is a modality of the protective instinct. It arises because of our instinctive

---

[6]   See pp. 70–72.
[7]   *Conf.* I I.XIII.I.

knowledge that a loss of the genuine love that we share with family members would cause pain in them, as well as in us. Our desire to protect a spouse or child from pain thus becomes a desire to protect our love, and this desire leads us to fear the possibility of doing anything to jeopardize it. Abba Chaeremon goes on to teach that the fear of God is the same kind of fear as the fear of damaging our relationships of love. This is quite logical given the fathers' understanding that God is love. The fear of losing love within a family is quite literally a fear of God's absence therein. Holy fear in a family, then, amounts to a fear that family relationships will not grow into the ideal of Christian friendship built on love, and thus will not manifest the presence of the kingdom of God within themselves.

Seizing the advantage of protective instinct, human love is given its greatest chance truly to resemble the love of God. When a husband looks at his wife and recognizes the anguish that she would feel should their love be broken, and when he desires in holy fear to protect her from this anguish, he seeks, by so doing, to protect her and their relationship from the anguish of separation from God. When, in the same moment, a wife looks at her husband and sees her husband cherishing their Christian love for one another, and desires to protect that feeling within him and make it grow, she does what she can to preserve their love, and so feeds a divine cycle. In such a moment, both know that what is required for the continuation of the love that they wish to protect for the other. They must give themselves up to each other in an act of their natural protective instinct, just as the mother bird, according to Abba Joseph, is willing to give up its own life to protect its young.

This work of mutual self-giving is the same act of humility that leads to unity of purpose as we discussed it in the previous section. In so giving of themselves, a married couple yet further increases their holy fear, seeing the spouse giving him or herself over and thus desiring to pick up the slack of the protection of the other's love. And on the cycle goes, if possible, into the infinite divine, one act of love feeding another owing to the fear of damaging each other's love. An identical movement of love through holy fear becomes present in parent-child relationships that are founded on love combined with the natural protective instinct. In sum, the protective instinct manifesting as holy fear spills over to become genuine humility, and thus unity of purpose, the keystone of a family's capacity to make manifest the kingdom of God.

This beautiful cycle, however, is impossible unless good works, compassion, patience, and humility are exercised in family relationships. As we have already made clear, natural instinct itself is not enough. The natural protective instinct operates upon existent love to fuel its growth—it does not make manifest this love to begin with. Yet, when Christian families *do* seek one purpose by practicing the key virtues as we discussed them in the previous chapter, the protective instinct helps them to become a powerful tool for reflecting and magnifying real love and building it up as a manifestation of the love and fear of God. In this way, family can become one of the most powerful tools of salvation available to the laity owing to the presence of the protective instinct within it.

Chastity and Sex in Married Life

In this section we discuss sexuality in a Christian marriage. We will begin by identifying the importance of chastity in Christian life, then observe the key difference that exists between a monk's way of pursuing chastity and a lay person's way. Finally, we will discuss some of the essential tools for pursuing the virtue of chastity according to the *Conferences* as they can be applied within a marriage.

The single most obvious difference between the life of a married person and that of a monk or nun is that, within Orthodox Tradition, married people are permitted to have sex. This permission has its roots in St Paul's acceptance of married sex as an allowance for human weakness. For Paul, a married life involving sex is inferior to the maintenance of virginity, but is not an outright sin.[8] The attitude toward sex in the *Conferences* follows Paul

8   See I Cor 7.25–40.

closely in this regard. In the twenty-first conference, Abba Theonas makes mention of Paul's teaching on this point in the context of a discussion about the difference between the demands of the law and the way of living a Christian life in the grace of Christ.

> So, the law mainly dictates that the union of marriage be sought, saying, "blessed is the man who has seed in Zion and a household in Jerusalem" [Is 31.9], and, "cursed is the barren one who has not borne" [Job 24.21]. On the other hand, grace invites us to the purity of continual incorruption and the chastity of a beautiful virginity saying, "blessed are the barren and the breasts that have not nursed" [Lk 23.29], and, "he who does not hate father and mother and wife cannot be my disciple" [1 Cor 7.29].[9]

For Abba Theonas (who generally has an even lower view of sex than most of the fathers of the *Conferences*), marriage, and thereby sex, are acceptable under the law, but the married life is patently inferior to the pursuit of a chaste life of virginity. This is indeed St Paul's message as well.

It may come as some surprise, however, to learn the reason that Abba Theonas gives as justification for the life of virginity being more desirable than the life of marriage. It is not, as one might expect, because he feels that virginity is itself an inherently more holy or honorable state. Instead, for Abba Theonas, the virgin life is preferable because it is simply more difficult, practically speaking, for married people to avoid falling into sexual sin.

> But under the law (in which the rights of spouses are respected) although the wandering of excess is restrained and subjected to just one woman, still the barbs of bodily desire necessarily survive. A fire to which fuel is added on purpose has a hard time being restricted to specific boundaries so as not to spread further and ignite everything it touches.[10]

Abba Theonas' point is not that Paul is wrong and married sex is a vice. Rather, he argues that those for whom sex is a part of life will

---

[9]   *Conf.* 21.XXXII.2–3.
[10] *Conf.* 21.XXXIII.2.

have a harder time—if not an impossible time—avoiding behaviors that are, without a doubt, sinful. He summarizes these behaviors as "adultery" and quite rightly so; for the teaching of the gospel is that even to entertain sexual thoughts about another person is to be joined to them as one flesh, and thus any departure from the spouse, even in the most fleeting of lustful thoughts, is a kind of adultery for the married person. In giving this assessment of the risks of married life, Abba Theonas is trying to prove a point about the nature of religious law, which he explains as follows:

> Therefore, the servants of the law slide into unlawful things by the very use of things that are lawful. Participants in grace, however, do not come to know unlawful things, since they shun even lawful ones.[11]

For Abba Theonas, the fact that God's law allows for certain behaviors is not necessarily an indication that engaging in these behaviors is the best way for people to live. One can do better than the law, and one ought to, he teaches. It is for this reason that the fathers of the *Conferences* join with St Paul in counseling that it is better to remain a virgin than to marry and thus introduce sex into one's life.

This implies something extremely important for us to observe. The operating principle behind Abba Theonas' words is that chastity is something that *all* Christians must seek. We see this in observing that Abba Theonas thinks that it is *more effectively* sought by abstinence from all sex, and precisely because his concern is pragmatic, he can only be assuming that even married people are expected to pursue chastity. Chastity is not a virtue unique to the lives of monks, according to the *Conferences*. It is essential to the pursuit of purity of heart for all people.

So, what is chastity? A brief quotation from Abba Chaeremon will help us to present an answer.

> Chastity subsists not in maintaining self-imposed austerity, but rather in the love of chastity itself and joy in the purity that accompanies it. When the opposition of desires still creates some

[11] *Conf.* 21.XXXIII.3.

level of resistance in a person, then this is not chastity at all, properly speaking, but abstinence.[12]

Abba Chaeremon's definition of chastity is revealed to us here in large part by his statement about what it is not. Human efforts not to give in to sexual impulses are not chastity. Works of resistance under these circumstances Abba Chaeremon defines as "abstinence." Abstinence from sinful sex is certainly good, but chastity is something that goes beyond it. Chastity, Abba Chaeremon implies, is complete freedom from the power of one's sexual impulses. It does not depend on not *having* such impulses (as the story of the young monk and the bad elder from the last chapter shows so well) but rather on freeing oneself from any level of slavery to those impulses that would otherwise dominate the human being. Given this understanding, it is indeed obvious that married people must strive to develop chastity just as much as monks do. Yet, for the married, the nature of chastity and the way we pursue it is a little bit different.

In order to see its definition for married people more clearly, it will help to continue thinking about Abba Theonas' teaching on chastity as the act of doing better than the law requires. We must make two observations. First, we must make clear again that his point here is a strategic one. Abba Theonas is counseling Christian monks about why it is easier (much easier, in fact) to cultivate purity of heart when one remains a virgin, even though marriage is allowed under the law. As such, married lay people essentially constitute a group that has decided against following the advice of Abba Theonas, and others like him, in this regard. We have chosen the more difficult path, the path of marriage that includes the presence of sex. This is a profound challenge, and this is our first key observation. A married life including sex is *not* a life relieved of a burden, but rather it is a life to which a burden has been added.

Our second observation about Abba Theonas' approach to sex is that in the passages quoted above, he does not seriously entertain

12 *Conf.* 12.X.1.

the possibility of being married and not engaging in sex with one's spouse. There are a few stories about such marriages in the *Conferences*, including one about Abba Theonas himself, and we will talk about them in the next section. However, here, Abba Theonas assumes that those who are married will have sex. This is what he means by "respecting the rights of a spouse." With this phrase, Abba Theonas indicates that individuals in a married relationship have a conjugal right to one another. The Mosaic law is clear in this regard, especially with reference to husbands who are not to deny their wives of sex, at least not completely.[13] For Abba Theonas, then, sex is basically a given as part of marriage, even if the presence of sex presents a tremendous risk to Christians.

Marriage *does*, however, offer some benefit in relation to the problem of sexual vice, according to Abba Theonas. Hopefully, he says, in married sexuality a person's "wandering [into] excess" will at least be "restrained and subjected to just one" other person. He seems to assume that this small benefit pales in comparison to the lofty heights of virginity but it is, indeed, something at least a little bit spiritually helpful. While marriage is a far more difficult path to chastity, then, it is not an impossible one, nor is it one that offers no benefits at all to the seeker of purity of heart.

A definition of married chastity in light of the teachings of Abba Theonas thus runs basically as follows. Married chastity has come to exist when a person ceases to feel the commanding power of any sexual impulses that are directed to anyone but the spouse alone, in sleep or awake, and when, by obvious extension, actual sex is made exclusive to the spouse. It does not require the elimination of sex, but rather its absolute restriction (in deed *and in thought*) to the married relationship only. This is a profoundly high calling, and a profoundly difficult thing to imagine. Yet, it is possible. How, then, is it pursued by married couples?

The best resource in the *Conferences* for discussing this is the twelfth conference, appropriately titled, "On Chastity." The

---

[13] See Ex 21.10.

twelfth conference is often a challenging text for lay readership, and much of what Abba Chaeremon says in it ought to be more or less passed over by married people. First, over half the text of the conference is devoted to a discussion of the problem of male night-time emissions, also known as wet dreams, and how monks can work entirely to eliminate these from their lives. A fixation on night-time emissions appears frequently in the *Conferences*, but in my view this particular topic is of very minimal importance for our purposes, not least because it affects only the male half of the readership of this book, and so we will skip over it. Lay readers of the *Conferences* may want to do much the same when they arrive at this section of Abba Chaeremon's discourse. Beyond the amount of the text that is devoted to night-time emissions, Abba Chaeremon's summary of the nature of chastity, which appears in *Conf.* 12.VII.2 and forward, is strongly geared toward the lives of monks who, as we have noted, have a different target in mind with regard to this virtue. When Abba Chaeremon discusses techniques for totally shutting down one's sexual impulses, these discussions are again of relatively marginal value for us in that we are seeking not to shut down such impulses entirely, but rather to direct them to our spouse alone.

Much of the rest of the twelfth conference, however, presents insights that are very helpful in working through how married sexuality can and should become a tool for cultivating purity of heart and thereby attaining the kingdom. To begin with, Abba Chaeremon places strong emphasis on his understanding that chastity, in particular among the virtues, is always a gift of God, and never something earned by those who seek it.

> It should be entirely clear to us that, even though we carry out every discipline of abstinence (hunger, of course, and thirst, as well as vigils and the burden of work, plus the constant effort of reading), still we cannot attain the permanent purity of chastity by virtue of these works, unless—while still doing them—we

learn by the instruction of experience that chastity's incorruption
is given by the free gift of divine grace.[14]

It is not possible, according to Abba Chaeremon, to work one's
way to real chastity. All the types of effort that he identifies in
this passage, while good and necessary, are not the same as chastity
itself—chastity is given only by grace.

This teaching is perhaps not surprising. There are few human
impulses more powerful than sexual impulses. It is easy to see why
it would be unimaginable to Abba Chaeremon that such exception-
ally powerful desires could be restrained by sheer effort. As such,
if we, too, find it impossible to imagine that we could, through
our own efforts, clear our minds of all sexual impulses other than
those directed to our spouse, Abba Chaeremon teaches that that is
because it *is* impossible to do so on our own power. Only God can
give us the gift of such chastity. We will return to the importance
of this idea momentarily.

The next important point about conference twelve for us is that
Abba Chaeremon teaches that learning to exercise chastity requires
that one seek out the practice of all the virtues together. Chastity
is not something that can be isolated from our struggles against
problems like anger, for example, but rather the work of becoming
chaste is an extension of the struggle for a life of purity of heart
more generally. On this point, Abba Chaeremon notes that "the
uprightness of bodily chastity alone is not enough [to produce]
the perfection of purity unless soundness of mind is also added
to it."[15] For him, chastity must grow from the other virtues, and
it does so when the motivations of the heart are totally redirected
from worldly desires to spiritual ones—when the human being realizes that the pleasures of purity of heart are more desirable than
the pleasures of the flesh.

> A living mind cannot carry on without some experience of desire
> or fear, happiness or sadness, unless these things are supplanted

---

[14]   *Conf.* 12.IV.1.
[15]   *Conf.* 12.II.5.

in a positive way. And so, if we desire to expunge bodily lusts from our hearts, we should continually plant spiritual desires in their place.[16]

Abba Chaeremon's description of what it really looks like when someone devotes himself to spiritual pursuits this way is very important for us here.

> However far someone progresses in gentleness and patience of heart, so far does he progress in purity of the body; and however far away he propels the passion of anger, so much more closely does he cling to chastity.[17]

Here, Abba Chaeremon counsels that patience in the heart will eventually lead to purity in the body. Elsewhere he calls patience the best spiritual medicine of all for the heart.[18] What is more, however, he focuses in the long quotation just above on the problem of anger specifically as a key impediment to obtaining chastity. For Abba Chaeremon, the essential root of chastity is not abstinence (though this is important), but patience and the absence of anger.

If this is true for a monk's chastity, it is even more so for chastity in a married relationship. The work of married chastity is begun not by focusing directly on the question of sexual impulses in themselves, but by the pursuit of all the virtues within marriage, especially including patience and the comforting of anger. This is because when resentment, bitterness, and anger are present in a marriage, they repel us from our spouses and create barriers to emotional connection and sexual intimacy. Indeed, most married couples are well aware of how conflicts over entirely different issues inevitably spill over into the bedroom.

Now, this is important because, if we are seeking to focus our sexuality entirely on our spouse, this goal is quite obviously impeded if there are barriers to our connection with that spouse in love. We must recall that married chastity as we have defined it is

---

[16]   *Conf.* 12.V.3.
[17]   *Conf.* 12.VI.1.
[18]   *Conf.* 12.VI.5.

not only about *not* directing our sexuality to other people, but also about actively directing it *toward* our spouse. We must recall, in turn, that for Abba Chaeremon it is the work of developing an active love of the virtue of chastity, rather than resisting temptations to its opposite, that really allows chastity to grow in a person. Thus, if we do not cultivate genuine love in our marriage through virtue, but instead repel one another with anger, we get in the way of the active process by which our sexuality is directed to one another in the form of married chastity. We cannot, after all, easily direct our sexual impulses toward a person giving us the silent treatment, or to whom we are doing the same. We cannot love the beauty of a sexual relationship embittered by anger.

The work of focusing sexuality entirely within a married relationship is thus only possible if both husband and wife pursue purity of heart through the virtues, and thus cultivate genuine love. It is precisely this order of operations that Abba Chaeremon teaches is always necessary for chastity to bloom, even for monks— virtue first, chastity to follow. This teaching ought to recall our minds to the first section of this chapter in which we discussed the importance of unity of purpose in the married relationship. There we noted with Abba Joseph that the virtues of patience and a lack of anger, which result in the giving over of the personal will to the spouse, are the foundations of unity of purpose. Here, Abba Chaeremon is teaching much the same thing with relation to chastity. Patience and a lack of anger grow into real chastity.

What, then, is chastity within a married relationship beyond a total unity of purpose that is, in this case, specifically exercised with regard to sexuality? Married chastity is one and the same movement as all efforts to unity of purpose in a marriage. In married chastity, sexuality is not eliminated, but totally united to a specific other person. It is not cast away, but rather given over, the will of the individual set aside such that each spouse's sexuality is devoted only to the other spouse and no one else. This sexual unity of purpose, like all unity of purpose, makes possible the presence of the kingdom of God in a married relationship.

By cultivating the virtues, the married couple seeks to link their sexuality not to the desires of their flesh, but rather to the genuine Christian love between themselves. The transformation in the mind, when this is accomplished, even in a small way, is remarkable. One begins to see that sexual desire need not be an effect of the impulses of the body, but rather can exist as something that is an extension of the unity of purpose between a married couple. One begins to feel a sense not even merely of disgust, but of emptiness when reflecting on sexual desires that are driven not by this genuine love, but by base carnal impulse. The arbitrariness of such desires becomes obvious in the morass of ever-changing depictions of what is beautiful and desirable. The meaninglessness of an attraction to a physical body without any knowledge of a person's mind or soul becomes painfully clear. The desire to possess other people as mere objects begins to seem what it is—insane and impossible. Animal impulses actually begin to disappear as they are replaced by a longing not for a particular body, but for unity of purpose in love. In short, to imagine sexuality without the kind of genuine love shared with the spouse begins to become genuinely repugnant to the Christian because it so pales in comparison to the beauty of married chastity. When this is accomplished, by natural extension, the problem of restricting one's sexual impulses to one's spouse alone begins to resolve not primarily through powerful resistance, but through the atrophy of any desire to follow them.

This chaste kind of sexuality in a marriage begins to build the same experience of the kingdom that all unity of purpose breeds. One realizes that the desire of one's spouse has a will and directionality of its own, guiding the married couple to one another, never toward anyone outside the marriage, and thus to the divine. It has a power of movement that sweeps both people up into something beyond, and, what is more, it is not stale with the air of fleeting bodily desire, but rather crisp with the air of eternality, giving the sense that it need never end, but can be forever, not merely into old age when physical sex will eventually cease, but even beyond death when the body will have no more capacity to lust at all. In this way, sex becomes not an act of fleshly desire, but a material testimony of a real unity of purpose between husband and wife, an act of patience, humility and genuine love. It thus makes room between them for the kingdom of God.

The procreative power of sex is perhaps the most astounding witness to its meaning in a marriage centered on unity of purpose and thus chastity. It can be puzzling to wonder why the work of creating new life ought to be attached to something like sex. In the logic of the world, where sex is always an act of lust, it makes little sense. The creation of life, perhaps the most sacred experience any parent will ever have, seems far too weighty to be linked to the mere carrying out of physical desire. Yet, as a witness not to the couple's physical lust for one another, but rather to their desire to cultivate the kingdom of God, the connection between procreation and sex seems something quite a bit more profound. Here, God works through each married couple to make manifest his kingdom, if they join one another in true unity of purpose. The kingdom, just as it becomes manifest in their love for one another, when that love is made physical by way of sex, also becomes manifest physically in the form of a new human being. Because sex is ideally an extension of the presence of the kingdom in a couple's relationship, its connection with the growth of that kingdom within the world is not arbitrary, as it would seem to our broken culture, but sublime.

The role of sex in welcoming the presence of the kingdom in a relationship is why it is so important for us that Abba Chaeremon focuses on chastity as always a gift of God. Married chastity is not attained by heroic acts of mental abstinence, but by the presence of God in a marriage—by the realization of the kingdom there. To follow the teachings of the *Conferences* thus requires the married couple to do nothing more and nothing less than to connect their sexual relationship with their Christian friendship, and to make their sexuality a witness to their unity of purpose and the presence of the kingdom. When, for the couple, sex becomes nothing more than a material witness to this kingdom, chastity has been attained.

Abba Chaeremon speaks powerfully about the indescribable beauty that becomes present in a heart filled with perfect chastity.

> In each case, as far as the mind proceeds toward a sharper purity, so much more loftily will it contemplate God, and it will conceive wonder within itself, bit by bit, rather than coming to an ability to talk about this or give any description meant to explain it.... It is like someone who wants to give a description of the sweetness of honey to someone who never once has tasted anything sweet.[19]

This is a beautiful assessment of the indescribable nature of God's real presence in a chaste heart. This presence is available to married couples by seeking chastity in their own relationship. Theirs will not be, and should not be, a chastity of total abstinence. Instead, they walk the harder road of developing absolute unity of purpose between themselves, and thus a real Christian friendship of love, into which relationship they introduce sexuality and seek to cultivate it not as an enemy of their unity, but as a witness to it.

As with nearly all aspects of Christian life, married chastity is likely to break down for most of us far more often than it lives up to its lofty ideal. Hopefully we transgress its bounds only in our minds, for in cases of actualized adultery it is unlikely that most marriages will survive. However, while we may be able to stay out of the physical arms of another person, we will almost certainly find our minds there from time to time over the course of our married life. We note this for two reasons. First, nothing said above should be construed to imply that married people should put up no resistance to any sexual desires that direct them outside of the marriage. Such impulses should indeed be resisted. It is only that we must recognize that the fullness of married chastity will not, ultimately, be attained solely through this resistance. Second, realizing that we fail time and again to manifest chastity in our marriages becomes, as we are now accustomed to seeing, an opportunity to exercise discretion.

---

[19] *Conf.* 12.XIII.1.

Indeed, Abba Chaeremon notes that sexual temptations can teach us not to become prideful about whatever degree of chastity we do achieve.

> Yet, until we are worthy to attain a peace firm and unwavering, it is necessary for us to be tried by many attacks.... After a lengthy period of purity of body—as we come to the point of hoping to have gotten past every carnal contamination—we notice the stings of the flesh rising against us again because of the pride in our hearts.[20]

Our sexual temptations, according to Abba Chaeremon, are useful for drawing our minds away from pride in the accomplishment of chastity. This teaching is consistent with his assertion that real chastity is a gift from God, and never something accomplished by an individual. If we fall into thinking that it is we, through our strength of effort, who have attained chastity, then our temptations direct our minds as to how far we still have to go, and how impossible it is to get there on our own.

As such, our breakdowns in married chastity must become opportunities to call our minds back to the loftiness of what we seek in our married sexuality: the kingdom of God. To see ourselves stumble must become a chance to recall that it is only God's presence in our married relationship that makes chastity possible. Recalling this, in turn, must remind us of how beautiful is the thing that we were seeking. When we return our minds to thoughts of the beauty of sexuality as an expression of unity of purpose, we will find ourselves moving once again further away from the mere physical aspects of sexual desire. Thus, when these physical desires do arise in us, they must become themselves a goad pushing the mind back to the memory of real love in purity of heart.

Married chastity, as we have described it in accordance with the *Conferences,* is hard. It is more difficult, in fact, than complete abstinence from sexuality and sexual thoughts. As such, the monks of the *Conferences* do not wish it for us. But, for those who are indeed

---

[20]   *Conf.* 12.VI.6–7.

married, it is possible, just as much as chastity is possible for a monk. It comes to be when our sexuality is directed exclusively to our spouse by being subsumed into our relationship of Christian friendship with husband or wife. When we are able to incorporate sexuality into our marriage in this way, it becomes a witness to our unity of purpose, built on genuine love. If our sole sexual relationship, that of marriage, is transformed into a relationship of this kind of chastity, it will indeed be a great tool for our pursuit of purity of heart, and a site wherein our *telos*, the kingdom of God becomes manifest.

Approaching Radical Examples in the Texts

There are certain sections in the *Conferences* that, in my view, pose serious risks to readers living in the world in that they are easy to misinterpret. Two of the most notable examples are stories surrounding the question of married life, which is why we take them up in this chapter. The first story involves a man who, with the consent of his wife, sought to establish chastity in his marriage by foregoing sex altogether. The second describes the life of Abba Theonas, one of the fathers of the *Conferences* whom we have quoted quite often to this point, who ultimately abandoned his wife to live as a monk in the desert. Both stories should raise some concerns for us in that either can easily be misunderstood by married readers to provide a call or justification for going to certain extremes in the pursuit of the kingdom of God.

The first story comes in the fourteenth conference. Here, Abba Nesteros relates the tale of a man living in the world who was spotted by a desert monk, Abba John, healing an old man of a demon that was tormenting him. Abba John, who had tried himself but had been unable to exorcise the demon, asks the layman how he had attained such grace. According to the story, the layman recounts that he lives a simple, pious life—always thanking God for what he has, and trying to do simple acts of kindness to others. This all strikes Abba John as fairly typical, and so, when pressed further, the man finally admits to something extraordinary about himself.

> The young man admitted that twelve years before, at a time when he wished to be dedicated as a monk, he was forced by the power and authority of his parents to take a wife; and without anybody ever knowing, he still kept her a virgin—like a sister. When the old man heard this, he was so taken with admiration that he declared publicly (right in front of the young man) that any demon was of good sense to despise this man and refuse to tolerate his presence—this man whose virtue the old monk himself (not just in the prime of his youth, but even now) would not dare to aim at without losing his chastity.[21]

Abba Nesteros goes on, in the very next paragraph, to make clear that the fathers did not consider this kind of lifestyle to be advisable for most.

> And though Abba John would tell this story with the utmost admiration, yet he never advised any monk to try this plan as he knew that many things which are rightly done by some can draw others who imitate them into great danger.[22]

Thus, Abba Nesteros is quick to note how unusual the lifestyle of the young man and his wife is. In this case, his concern is to warn other monks against trying something similar. The reasons are probably obvious—it is difficult to imagine most people simply foregoing the opportunity for sex provided within the bonds of matrimony; abstinence is not best pursued in an environment where sex is available, and even accepted by the Church.

But what of those in the world? Stories such as these can often give us great pause, and cause us to wonder if we ought to emulate this kind of extraordinary behavior. In accordance with the *Conferences*, it is clear that we should not. In order to explore why, we will examine briefly the even more radical approach taken by Abba Theonas. St John relates his story as an introduction to the

---

[21]   *Conf.* 14.VII.4.
[22]   *Conf.* 14.VII.5. Translation adapted from Gibson.

twenty-first conference. He begins by giving the background to Theonas' marriage.

> So, when Abba Theonas was quite young, he was joined in the bonds of marriage thanks to the preference and authority of his parents. They were looking out for his good repute, thanks to religious scruples, and were worried about a dangerous misstep at a tricky age. They thought that the urges of adolescence would be put under control by their lawful antidote—marriage.[23]

A similarity to the other tale of the young man is immediately obvious. In both cases, the men involved were forced into marriage by their parents. In the case of Abba Theonas, his parents appear to have made an error in judgment by wrongly assuming that married life would make the pursuit of chastity easier for their son. Thus, while well intentioned, they imprudently pushed him into marriage. We will return to this point in a moment.

According to St John Cassian, Theonas was living a married life when at some point he encountered a desert monk while on a short pilgrimage with some other laymen to give tithes in support of some of the desert fathers. On this pilgrimage, he heard a rousing sermon by an Abba John, who extolled the virtues of gospel perfection, and the importance of rising above the spiritual bare necessities required by the law. Inspired by the sermon, Theonas concluded that this principle should apply to his whole life, and came to believe that while married sexuality might be acceptable within the bounds of God's law, he himself was called to something beyond this bare minimum. He returned home and began trying to convince his wife to join him in leading a life of married abstinence exactly like that of the young man whose story began this section. While St John emphasizes time and again that Abba Theonas had no desire to abandon his wife emotionally or physically, or to stop supporting her, as he was doing, he is reported as saying that he no longer feels that sex can be a part of his life. Indeed, his disdain for sexuality is quite clear from St John's descriptions.

[23]   *Conf.* 21.I.1.

> Therefore, Theonas considered himself already in a state of duplicity if, after encountering good, gleaming, and heavenly things, he were to prefer the earthly and the foul.[24]

Sex, for Theonas, now appeared "foul" and far distant from gospel perfection. Theonas had come to see sexuality and salvation as mutually exclusive, at the very least in his own case. His wife, however, refused to pursue an abstinent path with him, despite extended cajoling on his part. Faced with the failure of his persuasions, Abba Theonas decided to abandon his wife rather than continue in a marriage that included sex, as she preferred. He quotes the Gospel of Luke in explaining this decision to her.

> If, in fact, you do not want to be a helper to me, but rather a deceiver, and if you would rather be a support to the adversary than to me ... then I will firmly seize upon the opinion expressed by Abba John—the word of Christ, in fact ... who, of course, says that "he who does not hate father and mother and children and brothers and sisters and wife and homestead—even his own soul—cannot be my disciple" [Lk 14.26].[25]

Salvation is more important than wife and family, Theonas argues, and so he must depart for the desert.

St John Cassian draws the tale to a close by noting that this remarkable Abba came to exceptional holiness and humility much more quickly than most. Theonas would go on to be one of the great elders of the desert, and the rest of the twenty-first conference is devoted to his teachings. Lay readers are probably quite shaken by the story of Abba Theonas. His disdain for sex and outright abandonment of his wife actually worked out well in his case, spiritually speaking. Are we called to emulate him outwardly by living celibate lives, and even possibly walking away from our marriages?

St John gives us the beginnings of an answer when he follows the story of Abba Theonas with the only real example in the

---

[24]   *Conf.* 21.IX.1.
[25]   *Conf.* 21.IX.6.

Conferences of outright consternation and hand-wringing about a given teaching or story. This comes in the form of an extended disclaimer.

> But let no one imagine that we have invented this for the sake of encouraging divorce, as we not only in no way condemn marriage, but also, following the words of the apostle, say: "marriage is honorable in all, and the bed undefiled" [Heb 13.4], but it was in order faithfully to show the reader the origin of the conversion by which *this* great man was dedicated to God. And I ask the reader kindly to allow that, whether he likes this or no, in either case I am free from blame, and to give the praise or blame for this act to its real author. But as for me, as I have not put forward an opinion of my own on this matter, but have given a simple narration of the history of the facts, it is fair that as I claim no praise from those who approve of what was done, so I should not be attacked by the hatred of those who disapprove of it. Let every man therefore, as we have said, have his own opinion on the matter.[26]

This is not exactly a raving endorsement of Abba Theonas' behavior, and St John actually continues the disclaimer for several more lines beyond this already lengthy quotation. The implication of what he is saying is that, at the very least, he has serious doubts about how good an example Abba Theonas is for others in this regard. Distancing himself from the story, he anticipates serious objections from his readers here, something that he never does in any other portion of the *Conferences*. In short, the story was rather disturbing to St John himself, and so, if we find it difficult, we are at least joined by him in this feeling.

However, St John does go on also to warn his readers against overly condemning Abba Theonas as an individual. His argument is, in essence, that because Abba Theonas came to holiness, it is difficult or impossible to criticize his particular path to that state.[27] The decision to leave his wife really was the right one *for Abba*

---

[26] *Conf.* 21.X.1–3. Translation Gibson. Emphasis mine.
[27] *Conf,* 21.X.3.

Theonas, St John teaches, and so, as far as the life of this individual goes, the decision must not be decried.

But, as St John's consternation implies, to uphold Abba Theonas' example as worthy of universal emulation would be a tremendous mistake. This is not least because it would almost certainly result in the Church's ceasing to exist with no new generations being born. Yet, pragmatics are only a minor question here. What is more important is the fact that the abandonment of sex for all is simply not the teaching of the Church in the first place. We are backed in this declaration by the Church's embrace of married life, including for most of the clergy, and we are reassured especially by the ranks of the married saints who did *not* live celibate lives, but instead produced and raised children, many of whom became saints themselves by following their parents' examples.[28] Indeed, the complete abandonment of sex for all is not even the teaching of Abba Theonas. We have explored his approach to sexuality in the previous section, and observed there that he counsels against a married life including sexuality because of its difficulty while refusing to condemn such a life in absolute terms. He himself thus has no expectation that all people will emulate his life, and, as we already noted, expects that virtually all Christian marriages will include sex in accordance with the Mosaic law.

Still, Abba Theonas' example is troublesome because it invites married readers of the story to be tempted to fall into despair. Most of us probably cannot accept an abstinent life within marriage, nor can we imagine leaving our spouse and family to join a monastery or become a hermit. What is more, we would be hard pressed to find an abbot, abbess or elder willing to let us do so. Yet, if Abba Theonas' life really exemplifies a gold standard of Christian holiness, how can we help but see our way of Christian life including, as it does, married sex, as essentially a waste of time, hopeless for our pursuit of the kingdom?

---

[28]   The Cappadocians St Nonna, St Macrina, St Emily, St Gorgonia, and St Gregory the Elder are all good examples.

The *Conferences*, though, are not texts meant to draw us into such despair, and they were certainly not written with the goal of persuading anyone to abandon the pursuit of the kingdom—just the opposite. As such, we must carefully review the stories of Abba Theonas and the young man to make certain that our interpretation of their message is one that encourages, rather than dissuades, our pursuit of God. The first key point to notice in this capacity is that, as we already stated, both men were forced to marry by their parents. This is to say that in neither case did they make a conscious and prayerful choice to pursue married life as their rightful calling. God's call, for both of them, was to celibacy, yet their parents, acting in arrogant self-interest and exerting their own will without sufficient consideration of God's desire for their sons, blocked the road to monasticism for them. It was a breakdown in the family relationship, and a failure to live out the teachings of the *Conferences* on family life as we have explored them already in this chapter, that led to the woeful situation of two honest Christians seeking to live the life that God desired for them. These are excellent examples of the damage that can be done to others, even well beyond their own children, by parents who fail to strive for unity of purpose and the kingdom of God through their relationships with their children.

Thus trapped by a their parents' spiritual shortcomings, Abba Theonas and the young man made radical decisions that really were the right ones for them, just as St John says in relation to Abba Theonas, and it is this point that allows us as married people rightly to understand their examples. We noted in the preface that this book is not for those trying to discern a possible call to monasticism, and we must reiterate the point here. I expect that present readers are in every case people who have discerned a call to life in the world, and most probably to marriage. That being so, we who are called to this married life must keep squarely in mind when reading a story like that of Abba Theonas that his call *was not* the same as our own. Considering this fact, not only should we not fall into despair when reading of Abba Theonas' dogged pursuit of the life God had always willed for him, but his motivations should be an example to us. It is precisely *because* we share Abba Theonas' desire to seek the kingdom that we who are called to married life must do anything but emulate him outwardly. Indeed, as Abba Nesteros notes in a quotation that we have already examined, "many things which are rightly done by some can draw others who imitate them into great danger."[29] Instead of aping Abba Theonas and the young man, we must pursue *our* calling to married life with the same strength and zeal with which they pursued their calls to abstinence.

Abba Theonas is quite right to point out that God's call sometimes puts us at odds even with those we love. It did in his case, and the results were heartbreaking, especially for his wife. Yet, he was willing to sacrifice his marriage, a marriage that never should have happened in the first place, because his call was to a life of celibacy. Are we who are *called* to a life of marriage willing to pursue holiness within that married life with the same level of commitment? If we are, this pursuit of holiness will not involve a celibate marriage, for this is not what God has willed for us. Instead it will involve our seeking of the kingdom *through* our marriage, including through our married sexuality in accordance with the teachings of the fathers, sacrificing all other goods and considerations in the pursuit of this end.

Among those things we must work most diligently to sacrifice, in this way, is our love of property and money. To a discussion of this topic we now turn.

---

[29] *Conf.* 14.VII.5. Translation Gibson.

Chapter 4

Property and Work

Vanity of vanities, says the Teacher, vanity of vanities! All is vanity.
What do people gain from all the toil at which they toil under the sun?
Ecclesiastes 1.1–3

While the desert monks renounced the ownership of virtually all property, people living in the world have no choice but to own things and deal with money. After married sexuality, this ownership of property is perhaps the most substantial difference between a lay person and a monk. Moreover, the fact of property ownership for those in the world colors substantially our relationship to work. While the fathers of the *Conferences* certainly engaged in work and labor, and discuss it frequently, they did not participate very deeply in the complexities of the larger economy around them. Instead, their work was mostly for the sake of survival alone, as well as for the occasional benefit of a brother or visitor.

Still, the fathers of the *Conferences* thought a lot about property and work, and their thoughts on these matters can help us to understand how owning things, including some amount of money, and performing work in a worldly context can become spiritual opportunities for us.

The Goal of our Approach to Material Things: Detachment

As with our discussion of Christian life in society and in the family, it is critical to begin our exploration of property by developing a picture of the fathers' ideal approach to it. We need to know what kind of relationship a person who has attained to purity of heart will actually have with their money and with what they own.

One of the most helpful texts in the *Conferences* on this point is the third conference, credited to Abba Paphnutius. Here, the abba discusses the importance of renunciation in the life of every monk. For him, monastic renunciation means, to begin with, the giving up of all property such that the monk does not own much or anything at all. However, for Abba Paphnutius, there is a lot more to spiritual renunciation than this. He identifies three essential kinds of renunciation.

> The first is that by which we physically cast aside all the riches and goods of the world. The second is that by which we refuse the fashions, vices and former dispositions of the soul and body. The third is that by which we begin to desire things that are invisible, calling our mind away from all apparent and visible things, such that we contemplate future realities.[1]

The first form of renunciation that Abba Paphnutius identifies here is the literal setting aside of all forms of wealth and resources, except for an absolute minimum of what is required to survive. The second two, however, are much more spiritual and involve not bodily and physical deprivation of resources, but rather the work of renouncing within the mind and soul first the vices (thus attaining to purity of heart), and all that accompanies them, and next all thoughts about the world of any kind. This third renunciation requires the monk to attain complete indifference about material things—a state in which the mind and soul focus only on divine concerns. We will describe this state as "detachment," and it is attaining this state that is the essential Christian goal with regard to material and worldly things.

Abba Paphnutius describes the experience of detachment in striking terms.

> We will deserve to obtain the true perfection of this third renunciation when our mind ... does not sense that it is enrobed by the fragility of the body and by a particular location ... but is taken by so great an ecstasy that it can no longer pick out the sound

[1]   *Conf.* 3.VI.1.

of bodily voices, nor notice the appearance of nearby things that we are looking at, but rather fails even to physically register large objects at hand, or huge items next to us.[2]

Most of us can probably only imagine entering a state of mind in which our mental focus is so totally centered on the divine that we cannot even really see the couch in the corner, or the table on the other side of the room. Yet, it is this extreme level of detachment that Abba Paphnutius indicates is sought by the monk, and there is nothing about his teaching that should lead us to think that he does not see the basic detachment that comes to fullness in this state as the ideal for all Christians, whether in the desert or not.

Here, then, is the first key lesson from Abba Paphnutius. Detachment is the goal of all Orthodox Christians, lay people, monastics and clergy. Those who wish to attain to purity of heart, and thereby the kingdom of God, must strive for a spiritual and mental state of absolute detachment from the material things of the world.

Yet, living in the world precludes a complete bodily renunciation of property, which, as we have seen, is the first step a monk takes to cultivating detachment. People in the world must own property in support of their own survival, that of their families, and that of the Church. Indeed, the ownership of property on the part of the laity allows for the very existence of most monks and nuns as well, especially today, since very few live off the land as the fathers of the *Conferences* did. We people in the world must own, yet we must also seek detachment. Is this possible in any way according to the fathers?

The simple answer is yes, at least in principle. To understand why, we must begin by observing that for Abba Paphnutius the first monastic renunciation, that of the physical setting aside of material things, is, in fact, the least important of the three, and is only carried out for the purposes of seeking the third renunciation of detachment. A monk who seeks detachment must focus on the

[2] *Conf.* 3.VII.3.

second renunciation—giving up the vices and attaining purity of heart—and, by way of this, strive for the third, in which he loses all concern for material things.

> Therefore, it will not do much good for us to undertake the first renunciation with the fullest commitment of faith, if we do not carry out the second with the same solemnity and the same ardor. And so, when we have accomplished this, we will become able to attain the third.[3]

Indeed, Abba Paphnutius is concerned that monks may get the false impression that simply giving up property through the first renunciation is sufficient for the work of attaining detachment. To make this mistake loses the point of renunciation entirely. He speaks of missing the mark in this way in the first person.

> Because, while in the fervor of the early days of my conversion I made light of the mere worldly substance (which is not good nor evil in itself, but indifferent) I took no care to cast out the injurious powers of a bad heart, or to attain to that love of the Lord which is patient, which is "kind, which envies not, is not puffed up, is not soon angry, deals not perversely, seeks not its own, thinks no evil," which "bears all things, endures all things" [I Cor 13.4–7].[4]

Elsewhere, Abba Paphnutius compares the carrying out of the first renunciation without following it up with the second and third to the forty year wanderings of Moses and the Hebrews in the desert. According to Exodus 16.3 and other texts, some of the Hebrews were known to complain to Moses that life had been better in Egypt where they had had enough to eat, even though they were not free. "If only we had died by the hand of the Lord in the land of Egypt, when we sat by the fleshpots and ate our fill of bread; for you have brought us out into this wilderness to kill this whole assembly with hunger."[5] In making this complaint,

---

[3] *Conf.* 3.VII.1.
[4] *Conf.* 3.VII.11.
[5] Ex 16.3.

according to Abba Paphnutius, the Hebrews stayed out of Egypt (which, for him represents earthly possessions) physically, but still turned back to it mentally and spiritually.[6] For Abba Paphnutius, the Hebrews in the desert represent those monks who have set aside all possessions in a bodily way, yet have continued to long for the things of this world internally. Such renunciations are meaningless.

> It does us no good, therefore, to embrace bodily renunciation (which is, on our model, a physical departure from Egypt) if we do not simultaneously obtain a renunciation of the heart (which is more sublime and more useful).[7]

Another point that we must establish here is that property, according to Abba Paphnutius is not renounced because it is evil. In fact, he teaches that worldly wealth is something entirely neutral, for example in a passage already quoted above wherein he says that the "worldly substance ... is not good nor evil in itself, but indifferent." The teaching that property and wealth are, in their essence, spiritually indifferent is spelled out even more explicitly by Abba Theodore in the sixth conference.

> But those things are indifferent which can go to either side [virtue or sin] according to the intent or wish of their owner, as, for instance, riches, power, honor, bodily strength, good health, beauty, life itself, and death, poverty, bodily infirmities, injuries, and other things of the same sort, which can contribute either to good or to evil as the character and intent of their owner directs.[8]

For Abba Paphnutius, Abba Theodore, and the other fathers, it is how one actually uses one's material property that dictates the way it will influence one's soul. Detachment amounts precisely to a recognition of the complete neutrality of material things. When we are detached, we do not start to hate material things (for this would attach us to them powerfully), but rather we disconnect ourselves

---

[6] *Conf.* 3.VII.4.
[7] *Conf.* 3.VII.7.
[8] *Conf.* 6.III.1. Translation adapted from Gibson.

from the deceit of the world that seeks to convince us that they are ultimate goods in themselves.

As such, what centrally marks out the life of the monk as different from the life of a worldly person in regards to property is not that monks have renounced something evil (property), or that their bodily renunciation is a virtue in itself. Rather, what differentiates them is that the desert monks have embraced a specific spiritual tool, that of bodily renunciation, for the purpose of attaining detachment. The monks of the *Conferences* have shied away from the fundamentally indifferent things of the world because, while these things can theoretically be used without any necessary damage to the soul, they remain spiritually dangerous and tempting. It is the fathers' implicit assumption, however, that such detachment ought to be attainable, in principle at least, without absolute bodily renunciation, just as it is their teaching that bodily renunciation does not always lead to the state of detachment that the monk really seeks. This approach to material possessions and the things of the world runs directly parallel to the approach to sex presented in the *Conferences*, which we explored in the previous chapter. Just as we noted that sex within a marriage is a spiritual challenge, yet one that does not preclude chastity, so too with property and detachment. In short, to return to the metaphor from Exodus, we attempt to stay in Egypt physically, while entirely departing it in spirit and mind. This is perhaps the greatest spiritual challenge that most of us will ever face. In the remaining sections of this chapter, we will explore just a few ways that the teachings of the *Conferences* can assist us as we proceed.

The Burden of Prosperity, the Blessing of Hardship, the Virtue of Balance

Perhaps the most important step toward detachment in spite of, and even through, property ownership, comes by simply developing discernment in light of what the fathers teach about the real nature of material prosperity, along with material hardship. In our world (as in the ancient world) it is commonly taken for granted that a life of plenty, marked by wealth, is good and desirable, while a life of poverty and need is quite the opposite. The fathers of the *Conferences*, however, frequently turn this paradigm on its head and teach that the comforts of property ownership can deceive, and eventually enslave us. So teaches Abba Abraham in the twenty-fourth conference.

> Yet, the yoke of Christ appears neither light nor easy to us, and this is because of our stubbornness. Cut down by despair and unbelief, we struggle (utter madness!) against the command (or, really, the purpose) of him who says "if you want to be perfect, go sell [or get rid of] everything you have, and come follow me" [Mt 19.21]. Still we hold on to what is material—to earthly goods. The devil keeps our soul bound with the shackles of such things—what else do we expect? When he wants to separate us from spiritual joy, he saddens us by reducing [our wealth] or taking [our things] away. This is what he intends by these clever deceits. When the easiness of [Christ's] yoke and the lightness of his burden have become onerous to us, thanks to the distortion of desire, and when we are tied up in the bonds of those same things—that same property—that we kept for the sake of our respite and solace, he will repeatedly torment us with the lash of worldly cares, drawing from us—from our very selves—that by which he tears us apart.[9]

Abba Abraham's words ought to ring true to any of us today, even more than they did in his own time. We lay people live in a world of near endless bills and expenses. The mortgage on our comfortable house comes due each month, and the insurance and the taxes soon follow. The car that was meant to get us to our destination in style now needs repairs, and the cost is higher than we had planned. We lie awake at night worrying if we have put enough away for our retirement, or for our children's education, both things meant to be blessings and comforts to us. In every case, we find ourselves lulled into assuming that our material goods all make our lives

---

[9]   *Conf.* 24.XXIV.1.

more comfortable, only to find ourselves working longer hours away from the family, getting snippy with our friends out of stress, and cutting back on our support of charities and the Church just to pay for them all. These are excellent examples of the devil luring us into a psychological trap with all this material. Soon enough, we become slaves to it, and this slavery takes a spiritual toll and draws us away not merely from God, but even from more important material things like our family, friends, and leisure time.

We have already established, however, that the fathers do *not* teach that material goods are actively evil. Abba Abraham's teaching is not that the ownership of property and things is straightforwardly wrong. Instead, he asks us to take a mental step away from our material goods and ask ourselves what is the real sum of the comfort they bring. The complex truth of the matter is that material things really do have their positives. As I type these words on my computer, I wonder to myself how writers ever managed to produce full-length books in past decades. My computer is a good tool and has a place in my life as a Christian. Yet, it is precisely the fact that material things are not absolutely evil that makes them so spiritually complicated and potentially intoxicating. The bait on a fish-hook, after all, really is good food for a fish—it is just that it comes with a catch. Abba Abraham invites us first and foremost to recognize the catch in property ownership and realize that our perceived comforts never come free, even materially speaking, and certainly never come without the risk of serious spiritual entanglement.

Simply recognizing this is a good step toward detachment. A person will be much less likely to become overly attached to his new car when he remembers how much trouble it will eventually start causing him down the road, the potential danger in driving it, and the negative consequences for the environment. It is not to say that he should simply not buy a car in the first place necessarily—that would be simplistic, and many of us (even most modern monasteries) more or less have to own things like vehicles. Rather, in seeking to develop detachment in himself, much good is done for a person by simply recognizing cold facts about the nature of material things in the world. If we do indeed determine that we must buy the car, we must do so with eyes wide open to the material costs. Remembering these material costs can draw our minds forward to considering the spiritual costs that are our real concern to avoid. It is, after all, only if the fish sees the hook that he has any chance of snatching the bait without being caught himself.

Prosperity, then, is a real spiritual risk. When we have a lot, we tend to be entangled in our possessions and separated from our pursuit of purity of heart. Yet, prosperity in the Christian life is not always all bad. Aside from recognizing its risks, it can also be used as an active spiritual tool if we are careful. Wealth, after all, can be applied in good works of charity, in helping others known and unknown, in assisting the Church, and indeed, in supporting our Orthodox monks and nuns themselves. This is no small amount of good, and without such daily efforts of Christian philanthropy, the pearl of the gospel would likely have been lost to the world long ago. Abba John, as reported by Abba Chaeremon, recognizes the spiritual value of philanthropy in the twenty-first conference when he accepts the material gifts of a group of devout lay people who have come to the desert hoping to support some of the monks and nuns living there.

> I am certainly delighted, oh children, by the pious generosity of your donations, and I gratefully accept the self-sacrifice of these offerings which are entrusted to me for distribution. By this, you faithfully offer your first-fruits and tithe for the benefit of the poor, like a sweet-smelling sacrifice to the Lord.[10]

The faithful gifts of these worldly people are a form of sacrifice to God. Indeed, we should be as pleased as Abba John about the good we are able to do with our material wealth.

Yet, we should also take Abba Chaeremon's comments, which immediately follow the passage just quoted, as a spiritual reminder of who we are when we give such gifts. For Abba Chaeremon,

---

[10] *Conf.* 21.II.

tithing and philanthropy are virtues of the law and the old cove-
nant—good works that are absolutely required of all people, but
that give us no spiritual pride of place whatsoever.[11] They are bare
minimums in the spiritual life, and those who live according to
such minimums are the last among Christians from his point of
view.

It is here, in embracing this status as the last among Christians,
that we see another way in which property ownership can be a tool
in the spiritual life. If we use our material wealth for philanthropy,
recognize the good that this does, and then remember that so long
as giving, rather than renunciation, is primary for us, we are in
the very lowest ranks of Christian life, then we can strike back
against the pride that material wealth invites in us. Rather than
seeing ourselves as the most important of people in the world and
in the Church, we can realize that we are her humblest and most
modest janitors—simply keeping the doors open and the sanc-
tuary clean for the spiritual growth of Christians. We, like Martha,
busy about preparing a meal, and in so doing we separate ourselves
from the teacher, and lose the better place of Mary. The job of
the property owner in the Church is indeed a job that needs to be
done, for parishes need roofs, monasteries need heat, priests need
food on the table. But the property owner's task is that of a Church
busy-body and grounds-keeper. By embracing Abba Chaeremon's
understanding of the spiritual place of philanthropy, we can thus
utterly invert our understanding of the place of wealth in our lives,
using it to invite ourselves away from pride.

Thus, material things are anything but evil for the Christian—
they are spiritually neutral in themselves and may become great
tools of philanthropy and even weapons in the battle against pride
for us. Yet, as we have established here, they can be deeply intoxicating. For this reason, the fathers teach that material hardship
can be a blessing in the Christian life. In illustrating this point,
Abba Paphnutius defines three different reasons that people give up

[11]   *Conf.* 21.V.1.

their property in pursuit of detachment. The first is God's call, the second is the inspiration of other people, and the third is simple hardship and poverty imposed upon a person by the outside world.

> The third type of calling is the kind that comes from necessity. After having been bound up with the riches and pleasures of this world, we are basically pushed suddenly and against our will toward God (whom we refused to follow in our time of material prosperity) by trials that assault us. Perhaps we are threatened by the risk of death, or hit with the loss or seizure of our goods, or pierced by the death of a loved one.[12]

As Abba Paphnutius continues, he implies that he expects his listeners to assume that renunciation motivated by need is inferior to the previous two kinds, since the first two types are voluntary. Yet, while he seems to concede that this is the case generally speaking, he is quick to note that forced renunciation through poverty or need can often do just as much good as voluntary renunciation can.

> Out of these three types, clearly the first two seem to be based on better origins. Yet, in a few cases, we see that out of the third variety (which seems tepid and low) people have emerged as perfect, and exceptionally fervent in spirit.[13]

The forced renunciation of poverty and need, for Abba Paphnutius, can spur detachment just like the voluntary kind, if it is approached with the right attitude. The reason it can do so, for him, is that it forces us to rely on God rather than ourselves, as noted above. If material loss turns our minds from what is fleeting in the world to what is eternal beyond it, then such loss is a spiritual blessing indeed.

While we typically react to hardship by assuming that it is a problem to be overcome, Abba Paphnutius teaches that to be deprived even against our will of material things can ultimately help us to gain detachment in much the same way that voluntary renunciation can. It can do so if we exercise discernment when faced

---

[12] *Conf.* 3.IV.4.
[13] *Conf.* 3.V.I.

with hardship in remembrance of the teaching of the *Conferences* on the nature of material things. Because we know that the ownership of property can be an entangling web and a spiritual danger, to be stripped of some of that property, even temporarily, must be understood as a kind of break from the spiritual challenge of owning things.

Do we see our material hardships as an easing of a heavy burden? For most of us the answer is almost certainly "no." Indeed, I suspect that inviting us to view tough times in this way is probably the greatest challenge leveled at us as lay people by the *Conferences.* But the very fact that we do *not* tend to see our hardships as moments of great relief can itself become yet another moment of opportunity for us if we are able to exercise discretion. What does it say about our relationship to material, after all, that we find ourselves suffering when faced with a relative lack of prosperity? Have we become too entangled in the things of the world to see how heavy they weigh on our souls? Have we placed our treasure in heaven, or somewhere else? If we find ourselves suffering over material loss, this experience should become, through discretion, a reminder of how far we still have to go in our pursuit of purity of heart, how deep our entanglements in the world continue to be, and how great our humility ought to be in light of these realizations. And, while many readers of this book may never know true and abject poverty, virtually all of us have at least experienced times when money has been tight, when worry and uncertainty has crept into our minds, or when things have turned out badly for us financially. Even if we have never been given the gift of complete renunciation, we do experience some degree of forced renunciation at least now and then. If we seize such opportunities through discernment and discretion, they will become a boon for us.

According to the *Conferences*, then, prosperity can often be a danger, while material need can be a great blessing. Yet, as we have noted already, neither of these states of being is good or evil in the absolute. The question is how we react when times are good, bad and in between. Ultimately, according to the fathers, to react rightly to all these things means to strive for the virtue of balance, cutting a middle way through the ups and downs of a life involving property, money and material. Abba Theodore teaches this explicitly in the sixth conference.

> Yet, regarding those who change direction with every single stroke of fortune that befalls them, it is said, "the fool will change just like the moon" [Sir 27.11]. On the other hand, regarding the wise and perfect, it is said, "all things work for the good to them who love God" [Rom 8.28]. Again, regarding the weak and foolish, it is declared, "all things are against the foolish person." [Prov 14.7 LXX]. For he gains nothing from prosperity, nor is he corrected by hardship. Indeed, it is the same thing to bravely face sadness with virtue as it is to stay balanced through prosperity; a person who is overcome by one of these is certain to hold up against neither.[14]

Abba Theodore goes on to say that rather than changing with her circumstances, the Christian must "go in a straight line, always walking on the royal road, never disturbed from a state of tranquility by the arrival of joy (on the right) nor driven back (to the left) by assaults of adversity and the power of sadness."[15] Thus, he teaches that to survive the ups and downs of the material world, the Christian must cultivate balance, and be swayed neither by hardship, nor by prosperity, from the focus on purity of heart.

Abba Theodore is quick to note that "it is easier for someone to be hurt by prosperity than by adversity."[16] This, he teaches, is because finding oneself in material need can sometimes be spiritually beneficial for the reasons we have already noted. Yet, while the spiritual risk of prosperity is more pronounced from his point of view, his teaching here is that *both* material need and material comfort stand as serious challenges to the Christian life. This is important for us because so far in this section we have focused on how to face the traditional spiritual challenges that material

[14]   *Conf.* 6.IX.4.
[15]   *Conf.* 6.IX.3.
[16]   *Conf.* 6.IX.4.

hardship and prosperity present. Yet, prosperity in particular can present one more kind of spiritual challenge to modern people seeking to live the Christian life. Counter-intuitively, for serious Christians, prosperity can at times become the cause not of pride and hubris, but of anxiety, self-loathing, and despair.

The reason is simple. In modern Western society, a good year, materially speaking, is one in which we enjoy a level of wealth that would have been almost unimaginable to the ancient fathers. Even the most affluent of ancients would have been dumbstruck by the kind of riches required to have hot and cold running water, electric light, a well-made mattress, a computer, a stand-alone house, and a car in the driveway. Yet, for us, these are simple marks of a basic middle-class existence—practically essential needs, not the luxuries of hyper-wealth. The whole scale by which we measure relative material prosperity is completely out of sync with the scale of the ancient fathers. If Abba Theodore saw the prosperity of a few extra loaves of bread as a serious spiritual risk, we may ask ourselves, how can we possibly survive the kind of material prosperity enjoyed by even a humble working class family in our world?

In times of what even we moderns call prosperity, serious Christians can be tempted to ask ourselves this question in a way that encourages the vices of despair and self-loathing in us. We may start to see our spiritual situation as hopeless, for we find ourselves neither able to function in today's world without things like electricity and a car, yet able at the same time to see the fantastical wealth that they represent. It can be easy to feel like Christ's words about the camel passing through the eye of a needle are aimed directly at us, and that, as a result, we have virtually no hope of salvation. Yet, if we have been called to the life of the world, are married, have children, and serve as supporters of the Church, then we cannot simply give up all that we have and wander out into the desert. As such, we can find ourselves feeling stuck and despairing. Tempted in this way, we may go so far as to give up on the Christian life completely on the grounds that there is no salvation there for people like us. Indeed, this is precisely what the evil one would have us think in such situations, and precisely what he would have us do.

What is painfully ironic is that if we do begin entering a spiritual state of self-loathing over our wealth, we can find ourselves not just far from detachment, but utterly fixated on our own material possessions for reasons *opposite* of the more typical and prideful ones we are used to. Instead of seeing what we own as a sign of our superiority to other people, and a symbol of our well-deserved status in society, we can come to obsess over all our things insofar as they are spiritual burdens to us. We can begin to over-do the work of recognizing the spiritual danger of prosperity. This is anything but detachment—it is instead a pathological entanglement that, if anything, is even worse than being drawn into pride by our wealth.

Yet, there can be little doubt that despairing in this way does not resemble in the slightest the kind of balanced endurance of prosperity that Abba Theodore enjoins, even if our modern prosperity would boggle his mind. Quite the contrary, properly to practice balance when times are good or bad will always lead us, he teaches, to peace.[17] If we see our hearts in turmoil and despair in the face of prosperity, we can be assured that we are not living as Abba Theodore would have us live.

How, then, can we live the life of balance that we should seek in face of this risk? The answer is simple, yet also radical in its own way. We must live within our means, whatever those means might be, and in so living refuse the temptation of despair and self-loathing in the face of our own prosperity (if it should come). When we have adjusted our lifestyle to reflect our means, while attending as we should to the needs of our community and parish, especially by tithing or more, then we have done what we can to locate ourselves in a material space in which balance can be practiced. Detachment cannot be achieved when we think about material things all the time, even if we think about them in order

---

[17] *Conf.* 6.IX.3.

to disdain them, for detachment, according to Abba Paphnutius, is the state of taking no notice of them at all.

Now, we must exercise discretion here and be certain that we do not cling to the things of this world and all our comforts on the grounds of avoiding despair. We must monitor ourselves to make certain that we are really just accepting our material situation as it comes to us. As the fathers clearly teach, there is danger on every side when seeking to walk the path of balance through a life of property. It is probable that any serious Christian who faces material prosperity will waffle from day to day and moment to moment between the temptations of despair and pride. We must struggle against both, and never let the battle against one lead us to lose sight of the battle against the other. Still, for lay people genuinely tempted to despair over prosperity, the tool of living within one's means and leaving the question at that is a critical one to recall. There are times for some of us modern Christians that prosperity must be endured not by self-effacement but with faith and hope in Christ's love for us and His reassurance that the impossible is possible with God.[18]

Let us summarize this section. Ultimately, we cannot attain detachment by rejecting the hand that life has dealt us, according to the fathers, but only by working to relate to whatever we have, much or little, in the right kind of way. As we have said, Abba Theodore's teaching is that both need and prosperity are things that come to us from the outside, spiritually neutral in themselves, and that it is what we do with them that counts. Everything assists us, he says, if we steadfastly endure whatever happens to us.[19] If we do experience prosperity, we must bring it out into the cold light and see it as a spiritually dangerous situation, yet still as something that merely befalls us rather than sullying our souls inherently. As such, we must recognize it as something to be endured with balance, and used for the work of philanthropy and humility. Equally,

---

[18]   Mt 19.23–26.
[19]   *Conf.* 6.IX.3.

we must not despair of material hardship, but must discern it to be an opportunity to disconnect ourselves from material things, and so to cultivate detachment by placing our hope in God alone. Buffeted as we will be by the winds of prosperity and hardship, the fathers of the *Conferences* remind us that through philanthropy, humility, discretion, and balance all worldly situations can be not merely endured, but can even become tools in our pursuit of the kingdom of God.

The Web of Charity

In the twelfth conference, Abba Chaeremon makes a brief but important statement about the nature of the spiritual risk that we face in owning property. In a discussion centered more broadly on the problem of fornication, Abba Chaeremon brings up the problem of avarice as well. According to his teaching, the spiritual risk presented by money and property is that it can be made into an idol by Christians who prefer it to the love of God.

> Whoever, then, does not give for the needs of the poor, and disregards the teachings of Christ for the sake of money (which such a person retains with faithless tenacity), that person commits the crime of idolatry, elevating his love of worldly material above the worth of things divine.[20]

We have already seen that, according to the fathers, worldly property is spiritually neutral in and of itself. It is what a Christian does with his or her property that dictates its spiritual effect. Here, Abba Chaeremon gives a concise yet profound assessment of what can go wrong with money and property. When it is preferred to God it becomes an idol. For those seeking the kingdom, this is an obvious disaster.

All this is consistent with what we have said so far in this chapter. What is now important for us in Abba Chaeremon's words is what he implies regarding the importance of charity. Here, Abba Chaeremon assumes that making an idol out of money and

[20] *Conf.* 12.II.6.

property is as simple as refusing to provide for those in need. He makes note that the earliest Christians held all property in common, according to the book of Acts, and in this way gave everything to charity and avoided idolatrous avarice.[21] In one short passage, Abba Chaeremon sets up two conflicting visions of how we may treat the essentially neutral category of money and property. In the first, Christians cling to their money and become idolatrous, veering from the path of the kingdom. In the second, those who are pleased to let their wealth go in works of charity, have quite the contrary disposition.

> We can see that many have cast aside their own resources for the sake of Christ such that we can conclude that they have removed from their hearts not just the possession of money, but the very desire for it.[22]

According to Abba Chaeremon, those who do not make an idol of their money attain the state of detachment that we have established as the goal of Christian life in regards to worldly material. Charity and detachment thus go hand-in-hand for him, while avarice and idolatry are similarly interconnected. To cultivate detachment, then, one must cultivate charity, which actualizes detachment in a concrete way.

It is probably not surprising to see the fathers juxtapose charity and idolatrous avarice, nor is it surprising that they expect those who wish to cultivate detachment to engage in charity. However, the foundational reason for which they connect charity and detachment in this way is perhaps a little less obvious. According to the fathers of the *Conferences*, the idol of avarice is damaging to the Christian because it is built upon a deluded understanding of the very nature of property and wealth. In order to make an idol of our money, we first must lose contact with reality, and fail to recognize a simple fact about all the things of the world, namely, that they do

---

21   *Conf.* 12.II.5.
22   *Conf.* 12.III.1.

not actually belong to us in the first place. Abba Paphnutius spells this out in the third conference.

> In relinquishing these visible things of the world, we cast aside not our own resources, but those of others (however much we may brag of having earned it by our work, or inherited it from our families). Nothing—as I have said—is our own except for this one thing: that which is kept in the heart, and is united with our soul; by no one can this be taken away. About such visible things, and those who hold on to them (as though they belong to them!) and refuse to share them with the poor, Christ says, "if you have not been steadfast with what belongs to others, who will give you what is yours?" [Lk 16.12]. Obviously, then, it is not only daily experience that shows that these things belong to others; it is also this saying of the Lord that proves it by his way of referring to them.[23]

Abba Paphnutius goes on to clarify that the "one thing" that he indicates really does belong to us is the virtue or vice that we cultivate in ourselves. Completely to the contrary, wealth and property do not belong to us at all, he says, no matter how hard we may think we worked for them, or how proud we are to have inherited them. To cling to one's riches, and refuse to share them with those in need, is to wholly misunderstand their nature. Remarkably, Abba Paphnutius implies that the best proof of this teaching comes from daily experience, and that the words of the Lord to the same effect amount to confirmation of what should already by obvious to everyone. We will say a little more about this aspect of his teaching in a moment.

In the twenty-fourth conference, Abba Abraham reinforces this teaching with a profound observation. Abba Abraham notes that for those in the world, everything that we possess comes to us by way of the charity of another, no matter what our social status or income level.

---

[23]   *Conf.* 3.X.1.

> Understand that you are affected by this no less than by the
> problem I spoke of before. Though your body is healthy and
> strong, nonetheless you are sustained by others—and that is
> something that ought to be the case only for the disabled. For
> so it is with the whole human race—well, except for the race of
> monks, who live by their own daily labors in accordance with
> the apostle [2 Thess 3.10]. [Everyone else] relies on the compas-
> sionate charity of others. This is true even for those who brag of
> being self-made, or sustained by the wealth of their families, or
> the labor of their friends—indeed, not just people like this, but
> even the kings of this world are clearly sustained by charity.[24]

Abba Abraham assumes that desert monks are the only people who
may really live by the sweat of their own brow.[25] His conclusion
here makes the point in powerful language, and we may well argue
that Abba Abraham has not even gone far enough. For, indeed, he
would have been well justified not only to say that "even" kings
survive on charity, but that *especially* the kings of the world rely on
others for their wealth, taken in taxes made upon the labors of the
lower classes.

This idea may not come to us naturally at first. Indeed, the
notion that we are self-sustaining and supported by our own labors
is perhaps the single greatest social delusion of our times. Here,
the fathers of the *Conferences* level a cannon at the entire concept
that the wealth that people in the world possess belongs to them
rightly. The money and possessions we have are not really ours, no
matter how lofty our status, they say. They always come to us from
someone else—they are always the possession of another.

We noted previously that Abba Paphnutius assumes that this
fact is self-evident, even outside Christ's teachings to this end in
scripture, and it should indeed be self-evident to anyone in our
society, Christian or otherwise. We need only reflect briefly to see

---

[24] *Conf.* 24.XII.2.

[25] Very few, if any, modern monks and nuns could make this claim, making
Abba Abraham's teaching in this respect all the more accurate and inclusive in our
context.

why. For those of us who work, and receive a salary or hourly wage for our labors, it is abundantly obvious that this income is given to us by an employer. What money we receive is not ours in any fundamental sense—it is given, and to say that it has been "earned" is merely to note that a particular exchange was prearranged or legally required. In just the same way, any income we might make on an investment, piece of real property, or other similar capitalist venture, comes to us by way of some return paid for out of the pockets of customers, tenants, or other investors, and often from the sale of things or even ideas that we ourselves did not produce, and perhaps have never even seen or understood. In such cases, too, it is from others that we derive our wealth on both sides of the coin—we sell the work of others (or sell God's creation itself) and are paid with money from other people. Beyond work and investment, we continue to live on charity as we do, of course, if we are on the receiving end of direct aid of any kind, either by way of any government services (from the use of a road to a monetary grant), or by assistance of a charity, friend, or family member. And, naturally, if we inherit something, it is another's property that sustains us yet again.

Thus, life in the economy is life in a massive web of charity, an observation that the fathers perceived as obvious. The movement of wealth from one person to another, which constitutes the economy, is always the movement of another's property, and no one in the system can rightly claim real and fundamental ownership of any of the things of the world. As such, avarice is an idol forged from delusion and misunderstanding. If we reflect on the fathers' teachings here for only just a moment, it becomes astounding to think that we could ever assume that any of what we have really belongs to us essentially. How could it even be possible to make such a mistake when living in the world—when every single pay check reminds us that what we have is not our own?

It is for this reason, then, that giving charity is so important for the fathers. To give of one's money in support of another is not an act of free generosity—the handing over of something that really belongs to us. Instead, it is the passing on of something that was never really ours into the hands of someone else to whom it will also not really belong. The giving of charity in this way amounts to an actualization of our discernment of the real nature of the things of the world. Conversely, to cling to our money is to deny reality—to fail to discern that our wealth does not belong to us. It is an error of delusion much more than it is an error of the heart. Avarice is not driven primarily by a lack of love, as we might assume, but by a lack of discernment.

For those who live in the world and own property, then, an enormous step toward detachment can be taken by simply opening the eyes of the mind to recognize the self-evident fact of our own dependence on charity. Every exchange of money and property, from the smallest transaction at a store to buying a home, is an opportunity for this recognition because absolutely every such exchange requires us to *receive* something from someone else, and thus be reminded that what we have is not essentially ours.

It remains important to emphasize that we must really actualize this discernment about property through concrete giving. It is not enough to be simply reminded by the world of how much we are dependent on others—we must freely contribute back again to the web of charity as a manifestation of this realization. We can do this at the very least by the giving of a tithe to our parish church, and beyond that the opportunities for charitable generosity in our world are endless.

This work of giving, in turn, helps once again to encourage detachment on our part, especially if we exercise discretion when engaging in acts of charity. Do we give out of a sense of obligation? Out of guilt? Because we think that it is required by God? Or do we give out of a sense of detachment and the recognition that what we have is not our own? We must ask these questions of ourselves because, while alms and tithes may well be given by a person who has not cultivated detachment, such giving, according to Abba Theonas, is very limited in its merit.

> On the other hand, there are those who still possess earthly things
> and only give a tithe of their produce and the first-fruits, and
> part of their income in accordance with the precepts of the law.
> Though a person like this might go far in extinguishing the fire
> of his sins by a sprinkle of almsgiving, still, however many of his
> belongings he gives away out of generosity, it remains impossible
> for him to be completely free of the power of sin—unless maybe
> by the grace of the Savior he sets aside his desire to possess things
> along with the things themselves.[26]

Three things are important to note about this passage. First, Abba
Theonas understands the giving of alms and charity to be required
by God's law. Christians simply must do these things no matter
what their interior state. Second, the giving of alms and tithes
without a heart of detachment has only limited value for Abba
Theonas, but it does have *some* value. As he notes, it may "go far
in extinguishing the fire" of a person's sins. As such, if we see ourselves giving alms and tithes out of the wrong kind of spirit, we
must not despair at this thought and cease our giving. Nonetheless,
and this is point three, giving alms and tithes only provides its
fullest spiritual benefit if it is done out of detachment.

As a result, when we give, whether it be to a beggar on the street,
to a friend, to an organized charity or nonprofit, to our parish, or
even to the government through our taxes, we must monitor the
state of our soul in so doing. If we see ourselves giving out of a
spirit of obligation, resenting the act of charity, then we must reflect on our own status as people who ourselves survive only by way
of the charity of others. Giving can, in this way, focus our attention
on our own delusions about wealth and material, and invite us to
turn again to see them in the cold light of the truth. Like every act
of receiving, every act of giving, no matter the context, can and
must become a moment of self-examination for the lay person.
Whatever our motivations, we must follow through on our charity,
yet if these motivations are not what they should be, we must also
seek to remind ourselves of the truth.

[26] *Conf.* 21.XXXIII.5.

By observing our dependence on others in the world, and noticing that we ourselves live only by way of charity, it can and must become possible for lay Christians, through discernment and discretion, to start seeing every exchange of money and goods as the passing between people of a gift already given and never really possessed. Remembering the web of charity when we receive, and when we give will guide us away from the popular delusion that we rightfully possess what we have. As such, these acts will help us to take a great step toward detachment as taught by the fathers, and thus toward purity of heart, which leads to the kingdom of God.

Work

One thing that is held in common by the lay person and the desert monk is the need to work. Between occasional visits from pilgrims who might bring food or supplies, the desert fathers had to labor hard for simple survival. As we will see throughout this section, however, the desert fathers tended to view work somewhat differently from the way we typically approach it today. Understanding how they saw work is critical if we are to turn our daily work into a tool in our pursuit of purity of heart.

The fathers of the *Conferences* view work as something that all Christians are expected to engage in at some level. For the them, St Paul's precedent is paramount in this regard. Following his teachings, they instruct that Christians ought to be able to earn their keep in the world, just as St Paul himself did as a tent-maker. In the twenty-fourth conference Abba Abraham reports on how St Anthony extolled the virtues of labor. Here, St Anthony is discussing some of the disadvantages of living in a monastic community rather than as a hermit. Among these are the fact that in a monastic community, one cannot be sustained entirely by his or her own work. Anthony explains that as a result it is harder to live up to the example of Paul.

> They cheat you out of the product of your own hands and the just wages of your own labor, not allowing you to be supported

by that which these things supply, nor letting you provide your daily food by your own hands in accordance with the rule of the blessed Apostle. When giving his last instructions to the heads of the church of the Ephesians, he recalls that while he was bound to the work of preaching the holy Gospel, he still provided for himself, and even for those who were preoccupied with more pressing duties in service to his ministry [Acts 20.33–35; 2 Thess 3.7–9].[27]

St Anthony goes on to explain that working to support himself is a necessary counterpoint, for the monk, to the duties of reading scripture and praying, and that the example of St Paul as well as the teachings of the elders show this to be the case. He does not immediately explain why this is, but we will start to get a sense of his probable reasoning by the end of this section. For the fathers, then, work is an important and desirable part of spiritual life, and so our task in this section is to discuss how. Our goal is directly to emulate their approach to work as much as possible.

For the fathers, work can only be a beneficial part of the Christian life if its purpose is properly understood. This purpose, according to the *Conferences*, is survival and, we may say by extension, support of one's family and community as well in our case. Work is not, under any circumstances, meant for the pursuit of the accumulation of material goods as ends in themselves. So teaches Abba Isaac in the ninth conference.

Indeed, worldly cares can still even come upon us, though we never get involved with the powers of this world. This is shown quite clearly by the rule that the elders have established. They define worldly cares and anxieties as pertaining to anything that exceeds the bare necessities of daily life and the unavoidable needs of the flesh—for instance, when working for one solidus is able to satisfy the needs of our body, but we strive to get two or three solidi by prolonged activity or more work.[28]

---

[27] *Conf.* 24.XI.4.
[28] *Conf.* 9.V.4–5.

The application of this teaching is a little bit complex for people living in the modern world, especially those with families. An urban life with children, the eventual prospect of their education, the need for continuing survival after retirement, and numerous other concerns, make it unwise for modern people to deliberately pursue the kind of hand-to-mouth existence that Abba Isaac recommends. In essence, when there are no fruits of the land on which to rely directly for one's life and that of his or her family, there is equally no way to avoid the accumulation of some assets in order to survive.

Yet, it remains possible to focus on excising the desire to work for the accumulation of ever more material goods even for modern urban Christians. While we cannot charge headlong into imprudence because of Abba Isaac's teaching, we can nonetheless continually check ourselves, through discretion, in order to examine what it is we are really working for. If contributions to a college savings account can probably be chalked up to "survival" as it has come to be in our world, an ostentatious mansion probably cannot be for most of us. We must ask ourselves the question of what really drives us to do the work that we do—if the honest answer is that we work for the care of our families, then we are well on the way to realizing Abba Isaac's teaching. If, however, we find that we work for continual material accumulation, then we must pull back from these motivations as quickly as possible.

The fathers also teach clearly that work must not be carried out in pursuit of glory and human recognition. In the modern economy, glory and money often go hand-in-hand, though certainly not always. We must be on our guard against working for the sake of worldly praise.

> We know that anything we have done with a view to human glory has been stored as treasure on the earth, according to the saying of the Lord [Mt 16.19]. Consequently, it is hidden in the dirt—buried in the earth—and plundered by various demons, consumed by the insatiable rust of vainglory, and devoured by the maggots of pride, until it is of no use or benefit to the one

storing it up. For this reason, every recess of our hearts must be continually scrutinized.[29]

Here, Abba Moses teaches that anything accomplished for the sake of glory will eventually be consumed by the destructive power of other passions. The wisdom of this teaching is easy to see in our world. An endless parade of politicians, executives and celebrities in the news every day remind us that wealth and power accumulated by people in love with human glory most often seem to be swallowed up and squandered eventually by the ever more questionable depths to which the same people find themselves sinking later on. We see the politician risking, and destroying, his successful career in order to have an affair, the famous musician wasting all her money on drugs and alcohol, the movie-star divorcing for the seventh time. When pursued for worldly glory, even the material success we do accumulate is most likely to be swallowed up by our other demons. How much worse will be the state of our soul in such situations? The antidote to this problem, according to Abba Moses, is, once again, discretion: the monitoring of which motivations drive what we do. If work is to be a valuable part of the Christian life, we must purify these intentions, and carry out our work for the right reasons.

We need to observe another point about work here. Just as work, for the fathers, is not about getting rich or obtaining glory, work is also in no way what defines a human being or gives life its purpose, as it is so often assumed in our world. Work, for them, is straightforwardly something that is done for survival. It is not the point of our lives, even if our work involves contributing to the betterment of society, nor is it for the saving of other people, nor for any other noble pursuit.

Modern Christians ought to take careful note of this understanding on the part of the fathers. One of the great temptations of Christians in our world is to accept the notion that what we do for work constitutes who we are in some way, a notion that

[29] *Conf.* I.XXII.2.

the world around us promotes endlessly. For many Christians, this idea is the driving force behind choosing a line of work that is perceived to be noble or altruistic. The Christian becomes attracted to teaching, charities, medicine, and other jobs seen to benefit the greater good. While there is no reason whatsoever that Christians ought to actively avoid such work, we must also refrain from making the mistake of thinking that these kinds of employment are spiritually more healthy for us than other types. The reason is that if we see our work in this way, we are very likely to be drawn into the kind of worldly motivations that the fathers so explicitly teach against. Instead of seeming to be something that is required to sustain us, our work can start to appear to us to be a glorious contribution to the good of humanity, on a scale large or small. Yet, to work for this reason is to work for human glory in a nefariously "Christianized" form. Abba Abraham points this out himself.

> And so, it is more advisable for us to struggle in steadfast perseverance toward the minimal fruit of this, our solitude (which fruit no worldly cares … can erode) … rather than to seek a bigger profit which, even if arising from the most productive conversion of many people, is still eaten up by the needs of worldly affairs, and the atrophy arising from daily busyness.[30]

For Abba Abraham, the simple life of the monk is far to be preferred to even the most holy of worldly labors, those that actually convert souls to Christianity! Such a view probably strikes us as extreme to the point of being questionable, but its meaning for our purposes is clear. If the perception that we are doing good for others causes us to become spiritually embroiled in our work instead of cultivating detachment toward it, then such perceived gains are not gains at all, but rather constitute serious loss for ourselves and even the Church.

From these observations about what work is for (and not for) grow the fathers' teachings on how work can be a spiritual tool in Christian life. The most straightforward way that the fathers of the

---

[30] *Conf.* 24.XIII.4.

Conferences sought to make work beneficial was by incorporating prayer into their labors. In the tenth conference, Abba Isaac recommends a short repetitive prayer that served as the most important predecessor to the modern Jesus Prayer, with a basically identical function.

> I must shout with all my strength: "Oh God, make speed to save me, oh Lord, make haste to help me." The words of this verse must be poured forth constantly, that we may be guided through adversity, and that we may be preserved in prosperity (rather than becoming haughty). Really let the meaning of this verse roll over and over across your breast. Do not stop chanting it during whatever work or duty or journey you are undertaking. Reflect on it even while resting and sleeping and attending to nature's call.[31]

Here, Abba Isaac points specifically to the time of work, along with several other frequent activities, as a time in which constant prayer is necessary and valuable. The ideal of constantly repeating a prayer during every waking moment is probably familiar to most Orthodox readers, and Abba Isaac's advice can certainly be applied by using the more familiar Jesus Prayer instead of the one he describes here.

The reason that it is important to pray continually during one's labors is highlighted in the twenty-fourth conference by Abba Abraham.

> And so, if our mind does not orbit the love of the Lord as its only fixed and unmoving center during everything we do, and during all our moments of toil, and if our mind does not adapt or reject a given attribute by the guidance of the right kind of compass (to coin a phrase)—the compass of love—then our mind will never possess (by struggling in the right way) the architecture of that spiritual structure whose designer is Paul [1 Cor 3.10].[32]

Centering the mind on the love of God is the purpose of continual prayer. While the body may be hard at work it remains possible,

---

[31]   *Conf.* 10.X.13–14.
[32]   *Conf.* 24.VI.3.

according to the fathers, to focus on the Divine, and so to continue to progress in cultivating purity of heart. Prayer fixes the mind on God, whatever the body may be doing.

Constantly praying while we work is probably the best advice one can give to a manual laborer. Indeed, for the fathers of the *Conferences*, work basically always meant the hard labor necessary to survive in the desert. Their teaching on the importance of continual prayer reflects this fact. Physical laborers know well the quietude of a day working with one's hands. The fact that the mind is mostly at rest during physical labor creates a vacuum that demands to be filled. For many in the world today, this filling is done with a radio or set of headphones, playing music or talk programs. Depending on what we are taking in, playing music at work is by no means necessarily destructive. Yet, the fathers counsel that the relative mental vacuum created during physical labor would be better treated as a spiritual opportunity—a mental space in which prayer can be pursued while the hands are kept busy.

To the extent that our work allows it, then, the fathers teach us to seek prayer while pursuing our labors. However, for a large (and ever growing) number of people in our society, work has long ceased to be equivalent to physical labor. The so-called "knowledge economy" leaves us increasingly bound to desks, telephones, and computers, sometimes thinking for a living, and yet even more *talking* for a living. This is, generally speaking, bad news for us as Christians. Mental labor is simply not very conducive to a life of continual prayer. We must focus on myriad other thoughts in order to perform our jobs, and very few of us are capable of the intellectual acrobatics that would be required to engage properly in a business meeting while also praying constantly. We should make one thing clear, then, about seeking to apply the wisdom of the fathers on work to life in the world: it is easier to do so for those who labor than for those who do mental work.

Still, things are not hopeless for white-collar workers, professionals, or business people. There is much about a life involving work, even of the mental sort, which can still be spiritually helpful, even if constant prayer is made impossible by the nature of such jobs. To begin with, it does remain possible to find at least some spaces in our work for prayer. Just as a physical laborer will often have to slow or stop her prayers to think about a problem, or talk to a co-worker or customer, those with mental jobs do have moments in which the mind is at rest, and such moments can certainly be filled with continual prayer rather than wasteful distractions. With enough practice, it can even become possible to pray while doing certain mental tasks and carrying on simple conversations, though this is not the place to discuss techniques for developing such an ability.

Beyond grafting prayer into one's work life, however, our very need for work can and should be an opportunity to cultivate humility, even for mental workers. The beginning of this process lies in exercising discretion about our motivations at work of the sort that we have already discussed in this section. Beyond this, though, recognizing the fact that we work to supply our needs also ought to lead us to the recognition that we *only* work *because* we have such needs. Our work grows out of our inherent dependency as creatures. We are not self-sustaining by nature, but rather rely on God and creation to keep us alive. The monks of the desert knew this well. Relying as they did on the meager food that could be found in their region would most certainly have reminded the fathers day-by-day of their total reliance on God for absolutely everything. Even the farmer, though he may do much to cultivate his fruit, does not ultimately make it grow, and that is to say nothing about the vast majority of us who are fed at the hands of others. To work in the world is to labor for something that comes as a gift from God—it is to be dependent on the divine, a humbling thought indeed.

What is more, for mental laborers especially, the fact that our work does indeed tear us away from spiritual pursuits much of the time should also remind us of our weak nature, and thus help guide us to humility. One commonplace in the *Conferences* is the expression of worry on the part of the fathers that people will become spiritually prideful, and lose sight of their still-broken nature and the need for God's salvation. In the thirteenth conference, Abba Chaeremon notes that tending to the necessities of human life (which is to say, working) can be a help in avoiding such spiritual pride.

> So, sometimes it is helpful when we perceive that we have been called away from these spiritual activities. For, when our focus is interrupted (against our will), and we must ease up a bit for the weakness of our flesh, then we may build up some healthy patience, even if unwillingly.[33]

Our need to work, consistent with the teaching of Abba Chaeremon, can teach us patience in the spiritual life, especially if that work makes prayer difficult. Such patience, as we have already well established, is the first step toward Christian humility. Unable to pray very often during the day, the mental laborer knows well that our pursuit of the kingdom of God takes a very long time, and the realities of life in the world get in its way. Yet the roadblocks that such workers face are themselves a reminder to avoid pride. We in the world who must work are the least of all in the Church, walking a long and unrewarding road that can only lead to salvation by the grace of God. Constant interruptions to directly spiritual practices should at least remind us of how inadequate are the dependent and mortal bodies we possess at present, how far our spiritual labors fall short, how great our need for God really is. Seeing our work as a sign of our reliance on God will allow us to create ever more space in ourselves for God's presence, thereby making work of any sort into a tool of humility and thus a help in the pursuit of purity of heart.

Concluding Remarks

For a working person, the owner of property, entangled in the web of charity and need, engaged as often as possible in prayer, pride ought to be utterly impossible, humility absolutely natural, and

---

[33] *Conf.* 13.VI.5.

detachment a simple extension of our discernment and discretion. Our work and our possessions, much as they really are spiritual burdens to us, can thus at least help to remind us of the foolishness of making an idol of the things of this world. If we allow property and work to teach us such lessons in accordance with the *Conferences*, then detachment will grow little by little within our minds and souls to the point that we, while living among all the things of the world, working for them, and even owning some of them, will nonetheless have no love for them. Our bodies will be here in Egypt, yet our minds will grow in the detachment that is essential to purity of heart and therefore reside in the promised land: the kingdom of God.

Chapter 5

Beholding the Kingdom

For the kingdom of God is not food and drink but
righteousness and peace and joy in the Holy Spirit.
Romans 14.17

Some readers may find it surprising that to this point we have not discussed at any length the familiar practices that give Orthodox religious and spiritual life its unique character—practices such as the Eucharist, confession, fasting, and prayer. This is by design. The significance and proper usage of such things is fairly well discussed in modern literature for Orthodox Christians, and our primary goal is to explore some of the less charted spiritual aspects of lay Christian life. Still, there is no denying the importance to the fathers of the *Conferences* of those basic practices that we tend to identify with Orthodox religiosity, and as such a book of this nature really cannot be considered complete without exploring them at least a little.

This chapter is by no means an exhaustive discussion of how the fathers of the *Conferences* approached the sacrament, confession, fasting, and prayer. There is far too much that could be said about their views on such topics, and, moreover, their teachings tend to be fairly clear such that little need be added in most respects, especially with regard to the various pragmatic questions surrounding these issues. Our goal, then, will be to discuss the theoretical relationship between Orthodox religious practice and lay life as we have presented it so far. We seek to identify and better understand the interstices of religiosity and life in the world.

One observation is important at the outset. For the fathers of the *Conferences*, things like sacrament, confession, fasting and especially prayer took up most of the day and constituted their essential work as Christians. With survival attended to, the desert monk turned to these things, and sought the kingdom primarily by means of them. The person in the world, however, cannot focus on these kinds of spiritual practices during most of the day. Attending to the basic requirements of life in the world, especially for those with a family, leaves very little time left over (as compared to the monks) for something like prayer, no matter how diligent we are about it (and, indeed, we should be diligent). The worldly person's essential work is *not*, therefore, to pursue these spiritual practices. It is, instead, defined by tending to the family, to society, to community—and, of course, it is the work of ... work—in a job somewhere, or in the home. Yet, there is no question that spiritual practices are expected to be an important part of life in the world. What, then, is their function in such a life?

For people in the world, religious tools are best approached as means by which we call our minds and ourselves back to our pursuit of purity of heart, and by which we remember and at times even encounter the kingdom of God, the *telos* of Christian life. The world is the real and ultimate arena in which we contend for our salvation, and our efforts in the world, if approached properly, are our essential Christian work. Yet, the world is also a place that invites our minds away from the right understanding of Christian life. It is a place that distracts and ensnares the Christian, and where we can often find ourselves, having set off with the best of intentions, on a long side-road leading directly away from the kingdom. Religious practices help direct us back again, and serve lay people rather like a set of side-rails and sign-posts for the spiritual life.

This chapter has been divided into two sections. The first, titled "Remembering Purity of Heart," will center on those spiritual practices whose primary importance for the laity lies in their usefulness for reminding us to continue seeking purity of heart. Here we will discuss the Eucharist, confession, and fasting as presented in the *Conferences*. The second section is titled "Beholding the Kingdom." Here we will explore the two closely related spiritual practices of prayer and contemplation, practices that call directly to mind a memory and at times even a kind of direct experience of the kingdom of God, and thus make manifest some level of encounter with our Christian *telos*.

Remembering Purity: Eucharist, Repentance, and Fasting

We spend a lot of time in life falling away from our pursuit of purity of heart. Yet, as it has been clear throughout our discussion, we are called ever to return to this pursuit. The fathers of the *Conferences* have plenty of advice about how to train ourselves toward greater diligence, and how to remind ourselves to return to our goal. Three of the most important ways that we can do this are by receiving the Eucharist, repenting of our sins, especially through confession, and by fasting in accordance with the Church calendar. We will explore each of these topics in order here.

The fathers of the *Conferences* talk surprisingly little about the Eucharist. Most probably this is because they did not all necessarily receive it with great frequency. According to one conference, many of the fathers of the desert were in the habit of receiving communion just once a year.[1] Physical distance from a priest may have been a barrier to some of them (most were not priests themselves), but it seems also that many abstained for these long periods on more principled grounds as well.[2] Whatever the reason,

---

[1] See *Conf.* 23.XXI.1–2.

[2] *Conf.* 23 describes a situation familiar in many circles of the Church today. Certain desert monks misunderstood the problem of worthiness for communion such that, out of supposed reverence for the sacrament, they virtually never received on the grounds of being unworthy of it. Abba Theonas rebukes this practice by noting that no one is *ever* actually worthy of communion, even once a year, and so it should be received every Sunday with a grateful and repentant heart. To receive it rarely, he says, is to be deceived into thinking oneself worthy of the sacrament on those occasions when one *does* receive it. This, he says, is a dangerous deception and so receiving too infrequently is a sign of pride in his view.

the Eucharist is a surprisingly marginal concern in the *Conferences*. Yet, it does come up as a topic of consideration in the twenty-third conference, delivered by Abba Theonas.

Abba Theonas' words about communion come in the context of a discussion on sinlessness and purity. He teaches that no one is ever without sin, and any thought that we have become truly pure is a delusion. In fact, the more pure we *actually* become in the Christian life, the less pure we appear in our own eyes.

> The more pure a person becomes in mind, the more unclean he sees himself to be; he discovers reasons for greater humility rather than pride. However quickly he approaches higher things, so much farther above does he realize them to be.[3]

Here, Abba Theonas identifies a paradox in the experience of those who pursue purity of heart. As they approach this goal, they increasingly realize their distance from it. It is a strange kind of target indeed that is ever more distant as it nears. Yet, the infinitude of God's holiness and purity are manifest in our experience here. Our growth in purity of heart is not a task with a specific end-point, but rather amounts to an eternal approach of the ultimate divine whose holiness will forever be infinitely greater than our own. As such, seeking purity of heart never ends, for the Christian—we do not *arrive* at our goal, but remain eternally dynamic creatures pursuing it forever.

Still, the paradox of the experience of pursuing purity of heart is a spiritual problem in many ways. Two basic traps are apparent. First, it is quite possible to allow our humble realizations of our own sin to turn into outright despair, and thus to give up our pursuit of purity of heart. Second, we can lose sight of our unworthiness and lack of purity, and delude ourselves into thinking we have "arrived" at the goal in a once-for-all sense. In such a situation, again, we give up its pursuit.

For Abba Theonas, the value of the Eucharist is found in part in the fact that it mitigates against both of these problems. First,

---

[3]   *Conf.* 23.XIX.3–4.

it precludes, or should preclude, any thought that we have arrived at the goal of purity of heart. For Abba Theonas, it is taken for granted that if communion is not approached in a humble spirit, it should never be received at all. If a person considers himself worthy of communion, he is by definition not worthy of it.[4] As such, the Christian must approach communion with the recognition that he has no business approaching communion. Doing so ought to make it impossible to delude ourselves into thinking that we have arrived at purity of heart.

Yet, conversely, the more one realizes his total unworthiness of the cup, the more he must receive the Eucharist according to Abba Theonas. As such, when we do approach it, it is also paradoxically a witness to God's grace and capacity to heal our souls, and therefore an antidote to the first problem noted above, namely, any temptation to despair at the thought of attaining purity of heart.

> Still, we must not abstain entirely from the Lord's communion because we know that we are sinners. Rather, we must hurry to it more and more eagerly as a ready therapy for our souls, and as purification for our spirit. Yet, we should do this with such humility of mind and such fervor that, though we judge ourselves unfit to receive such grace, we still seek it out as an effective cure for our weakness.[5]

To receive communion means, in part, to make material testimony to our faith in God's ability to heal and purify us, and our recognition that we have not yet arrived at this goal.

In a world where we are constantly invited to both pride and despair, and thereby away from the pursuit of purity of heart, receiving the Eucharist is thus a critical way to remind ourselves of our commitment to the Christian goal. We neither accept the notion that purity of heart is impossible for us sinners, nor do we rest content that we have arrived at it fully as yet. Humbly receiving communion drives us back to our hopeful, and yet forever

---

[4]   *Conf.* 23.XXI.2.
[5]   *Conf.* 23.XXI.1.

incomplete, pursuit of purity of heart. It is a critical sign-post on the way.[6]

If receiving the Eucharist serves as a renewal of our commitment to the essential Christian goal, confession does much the same. Abba Moses talks at length about confession in the second conference. To begin with, confession, for him, is a critical practice because when sins and passions are given voice, they hold substantially less sway over us.

> At the instant that it is revealed, a wrong thought grows weaker. Even before discretion puts him to trial, the disgusting snake begins to flee from his dark underground cave into the light—drawn forth like this by confession. He is sent away and disgraced; his poisonous influences reign in us only as long as they are hidden away in our hearts.[7]

For Abba Moses, confession is most importantly about opening up the mind to the scrutiny of another Christian person. To open the mind in this way helps, by its very nature, to mitigate against the power of sin by bringing our feelings out into the clear air. As he says here, the power of confession is already manifest even before we begin to reflect on the sins we have confessed by exercising discretion. To give voice to our failings takes most of the wind out of their sails immediately.

While simply acknowledging sin is the most critical thing about confession, Abba Moses also clearly teaches that confession is meant to help the Christian develop humility, and thereby begin to learn discernment.

> True discernment, he said, is only acquired by true humility. The first sign of such humility comes when both everything one plans to do and everything one thinks are submitted to the elders for

---

[6]   It is important to reiterate that this is only a brief discussion of one aspect of the importance of Communion in lay life, and not meant to present any contrast to the sacrament's profound mystical dimensions.

[7]   *Conf.* 2.X.2.

examination, this done to the point that, thinking nothing of his own judgment, one yields to their guidance in everything.[8]

As we noted in chapter one, discernment is most essentially the virtue by which the Christian avoids falling into intellectual errors, whether outright theological heresies, or simply bad spiritual teachings and advice. As we also noted there, discernment is attained, according to the fathers, only when the Christian learns not to trust her own judgments too much, but instead submits them to the judgments of those wiser and further along in the pursuit of the kingdom. Here, Abba Moses teaches explicitly that a form of confession is a critical way of actively carrying out the work of developing such discernment by talking straightforwardly with one of the elders who can help guide a monk in this way.

If using confession as an opportunity to get advice from more experienced guide was critical for desert monks, then it is even more important for lay people. In our lives in the world, we encounter very few people who can serve as real elders for us. In confession we seek to develop a relationship with at least one person who can offer a check on our own intellectual whims, and thus help us to cultivate the discernment required to navigate a world of misleading ideas and outright lies. If we ignore this opportunity and seek to walk the Christian path entirely on our own, we are obviously far more susceptible to being guided astray by our own thinking, our own mistakes, and our own sins.

By extension, confession is most important for us as lay people when we have fallen from our pursuit of purity of heart in ways that we ourselves may not properly see. The keen eyes of a good confessor often help us to think about our failings in different terms, notice those failings we have forgotten, and renew our struggle against the ones that we see. Through all this, the confessor helps guide us back to our goal. As such, confession is perhaps the most straightforward of all spiritual sign-posts in the life of a lay person. Having someone assist in the work of identifying the

---

[8]   *Conf.* 2.X.1.

specific particulars of our straying from the path, and offer concrete advice for returning to it, is a practice so obviously beneficial to the Christian that it needs no further defense or explanation.

Now, one thing that is very important to observe about Abba Moses' teaching on confession is that, following on the passages quoted above, he spends much of the remainder of the conference talking about the problem of bad elders in the desert, and all the spiritual damage that they can do. We have already examined the key story that Abba Moses tells about such elders in chapter two.[9] You will recall that the story involved a bad elder who was painfully stung by the same sins as a young monk whom he had rebuked after a confession. Thus, while starting off by expressing the importance of confession, in the second conference, Abba Moses ends up talking most extensively about how it can go wrong. He concludes by saying that the mere age of a person, and the length of his (or her) spiritual struggle is not sufficient commendation for his advice.

> As such, we must not follow in the footsteps or traditions of— nor take the advice of—every single old man who has a head covered in gray and nothing more than longevity to recommend him. Rather, we should follow only the ones we find who distinguished themselves during their youth by honor and decency, and who are steeped in the traditions of the elders, rather than in their own presumptuous opinions.[10]

The problem of bad elders looms large in Abba Moses' eyes, and the outward signs of wisdom that one might take for granted are of limited value to him. Yet, Abba Moses constructs this problem in a particular way that is important for us to observe. The worst thing about bad elders, for him, is not mainly that they hurt people directly with their bad advice, but that they might frighten Christians away completely from confession and all its spiritual benefits. As

---

[9]   See pp. 70–72.
[10]   *Conf.* 2.XIII.2.

such, Abba Moses counsels perseverance in confession despite the serious problem of bad elders in the desert.

> And so, never allow the inexperience or vapidity of one old man (or several) block or divert you from that sound path about which we have been speaking [confession], or from the traditions of the fathers; our most clever enemy uses their gray hair to deceive young men. No, everything should be confessed to the elders without covering or distortion, and cures for our weakness—along with examples for our life and conduct—should be accepted from them.[11]

Here, Abba Moses keenly observes that receiving bad advice or a rebuke in the face of temptation from a bad elder might well cause a monk to become gun-shy and embarrassed about confessing his thoughts and sins openly. Yet, he teaches that the monk must confess regardless of this, even if he has been burned more than once, and asserts that the practice of confession will continue to offer healing and a good example of Christian life no matter how many bad elders one might encounter.

Thus, while promoting confession as a critical sign-post on the way to purity of heart, Abba Moses simultaneously downplays the role of the confessor in a certain way. For Abba Moses, getting bad advice in a confession is no reason to discontinue the practice, because bringing one's thoughts and sins out into the light remains non-negotiable for overcoming them. He assumes that one will seek out *good* elders in the end, but having a good elder is not a prerequisite of confession, and one can surmise from his words that even if the Christian spent an entire lifetime seeking out a person capable of offering wisdom, Abba Moses would insist that they keep confessing to someone regularly all the while. If a good confessor gives an excellent sign-post back to purity of heart through wisdom and advice, the act of confessing even to the worst of confessors is a sign-post unto itself and thus remains critical in the Christian life.

---

[11] *Conf.* 2.XIII.12.

In light of Abba Moses' teaching, lay Christians must be mindful of two things. First, we must not be deceived into thinking we can walk the road to purity of heart without anyone else's help. We need real people to give us real advice if we are going to see clearly what is required of us. Yet, and this is our second point, finding a really worthy confessor in the world is very much a challenge. Indeed, most Orthodox Christians will simply give confession to their parish priest, whoever he may happen to be. Such a priest may turn out to be a wonderful confessor, but he also may not. He may struggle to understand our native language in some cases, may at times be too harsh or too lenient, may show very little insight into our personality or the kinds of advice we need in a given moment, or we may simply not get along terribly well with him. As much as a lay person's confessor may be determined by chance, however, and may be a far cry from a great desert father, Abba Moses encourages us to persevere in confession. This could mean simply suffering through with a parish priest who is less than ideal, or, as Abba Moses implies is perfectly acceptable, it may mean seeking out a spiritual father or mother actively. Whichever choice we make, we must never lose faith in the power of the act of confession itself. Confessing even to the worst of elders is a spiritual boon to us as lay Christians because, if absolutely nothing else, the work of confession *in itself* reminds us continually to turn back to our pursuit of purity of heart.

There is one more sign-post on the road to purity of heart that greatly occupied the fathers of the desert, namely, fasting. Fasting comes up frequently in the *Conferences*, usually with an eye to understanding the reason that monks need to fast, or to discuss some of the details about how and when to do so. Throughout the course of these discussions, the fathers make clear that fasting is a spiritual tool, never an end in itself. Abba Theonas lists it among those things that do some spiritual good, but can also be left out—"indifferent" things like marriage, or wealth, or even monastic solitude.[12] Still, while not a good in itself, fasting was nonetheless a critical part of life in the desert.

For the fathers, fasting, and other bodily practices, are necessary because of the material nature of many sins. While we can fall mentally in a large number of ways (such as growing angry, or prideful) much of what constitutes sin invites us to carry out some physical behavior in order for it to be actualized. For the fathers, gluttony, which drives us to the desire of food, is the most essential example of this kind of sin, and is, in fact, the prototype of all sin since it was by a wrong act of eating that Adam fell.[13] Because of the material nature of sins like gluttony, Abba Serapion teaches in the fifth conference that they require not just a spiritual but also a material response if they are to be combated—both body and soul need to be involved in overcoming them.[14] By way of fasting, then, the Christian makes her response to sin equally as material as her sins themselves—battling like with like. It is therefore easy to see why the fathers classed fasting as "obviously indifferent" in itself, while also considering it profoundly important.

For the fathers, it is critical that fasting be tempered with balance. Lay people, most of whom typically struggle against the temptation to neglect the work of fasting, may find it surprising that much of the discussion in the *Conferences* about fasting with balance centers on the problem of monks who fast too much or too sternly. By doing so, such monks are puffed up with pride, or fail to carry out the basic duties of hospitality when they are visited by a brother or pilgrim. Abba Theonas even says that fasting can be outright "vain" and "despicable" if done in the wrong way or for the wrong reasons.[15] In the second conference, Abba Moses gives a basic picture of how to fast with balance.

> This is the general norm for abstinence. According to his capacity of strength, health, and age, everyone allows himself as much as

---

[12]   *Conf.* 21.XIV.2.
[13]   *Conf.* 5.IV.1–3.
[14]   *Conf.* 5.IV.3.
[15]   *Conf.* 21.XIV.7.

he needs for the maintenance of the flesh (and not for the desire to stuff himself). For, on either side, a person can suffer serious injury, and he will do so if he waffles between squeezing his stomach by maintaining an immoderate fast, and then stretching it with too much food.[16]

For the fathers, balance in fasting means avoiding any temptation to be so harsh as to really damage the body (or neglect a brother as numerous other comments make clear), as well as any impulse to go lax and thus slide into vice.

Yet, the vision of balance in fasting that the *Conferences* describes as normal would probably strike virtually all modern lay people (and probably even most modern monastics) as almost impossibly harsh. Abba Moses, in conference two, reports that the teaching that monks should seek balance by allowing themselves two loaves of bread in a single day (about a pound each) seemed to him not even to be a real form of abstinence—he cannot imagine eating that much![17] Along the same lines, in the eighth conference St John Cassian himself describes in beautiful detail a meal that he and St Germanus enjoyed in the home of one of the elders following the liturgy on a Sunday. St John's point in the passage we are about to examine is to emphasize how far out of his way one of the fathers (Abba Serenus) went to make his guests feel comfortable by feeding them well. For St John, this is a mark of Abba Serenus' humility since he saw no reason to show off his usual harsh abstinence with visitors. Yet, the supposedly lavish meal strikes a modern reader as scarcely a light snack.

> We went back to the cell of the old man [Abba Serenus] and right away we were fed lavishly. For instead of the brine spread over a drop of oil that usually sufficed for daily refreshment, a bit of fish-sauce was mixed and poured over more oil than is had in a typical serving.... Then he set out a pinch of salt, and three olives each. After this, he brought out a basket containing ground chickpeas (what they call *trogalia*), from which we took five small pieces,

16   *Conf.* 2.XXII.1.
17   Conf. 2.XX.

two prunes, and one fig per person. For anyone in that desert is considered guilty if he exceeds this much.[18]

A few small fruits, chickpeas and a little extra sauce is, for St John, a veritable feast—the absolute largest conceivable meal for a monk before flat-out gluttony takes over.

In comparison to such descriptions of balance among the monks in the desert, even the most diligent of fasts by modern lay Orthodox Christians resembles a wanton smörgåsbord. When the lay person sits down to his bowl of lentil soup and hunk of bread on a Friday evening, he consumes a feast so large that many of the fathers in the desert, it seems, could not possibly have eaten it all even if they had wanted to. The fast of the lay person would be, to the fathers of the *Conferences*, a festival of incomprehensible consumption; it is perhaps best not even to think about what they would have made of our typical diet when *not* fasting.

We bring this up to make a simple point. From the point of view of the desert fathers, modern lay Orthodox Christians basically never *really* fast at all. At the very most, among the pious who are sufficiently healthy, there may be a few days of the year (perhaps clean Monday, good Friday, Holy Saturday, and the Beheading of St John) in which we genuinely fast in a way that approaches the fathers of the *Conferences*—truly eating the kinds of meager portions that they describe as noble. And, indeed, many deeply devout Orthodox Christians for all manner of good reasons, such as the limitations of health or the nature of their work, cannot manage even one such day in the year. In general, we laity have done well when we succeed in abstaining from meat, dairy, wine, and oil in accordance with the Church calendar. Yet, this kind of fasting has almost no resemblance to the ascetic feats of the desert.

What is more, lay people really *cannot* fast like desert monks and still function in even the barest sense in the world, and we would almost certainly fail in our calling as Christians if we were to try and do so. The difference between the layman and the desert

[18] *Conf.* 8.1.1–2.

hermit does not derive from some laziness or lack of care on the part of the layman, at least not necessarily. Our labor or mental work, chasing after children, keeping clean the house, tending to the grounds of a parish, singing with the choir on Sunday morning, and whatever else it is that we do—all these things require energy and health of body. It is of no benefit to us as Christians to pass out behind the wheel of a car because we have eaten nothing but a few figs for three days running, or to let the local church fall into disrepair because we have no strength to keep it clean. As pious and devoted as a lay person may be, he cannot live on two small loaves of bread a day, and he must not try to do so.

This highlights something important about the role of fasting in lay life. For the fathers of the *Conferences*, the purpose of strict fasting is to cut off bodily urges toward vice by restraining the desires of the stomach. Hunger and eating are not in themselves sinful, which is precisely why denying oneself food is a useful material exercise for those trying to learn to deny sinful impulses as well. As Abba Serapion says in the fifth conference, whoever is unable to resist simple pleasures like food will have no chance of grappling successfully with deeper desires.[19] What he means by this is that restraining one's eating is a relatively simple and easy physical exercise, and this is exactly why it is the best place to begin in the material battle against sin. Yet, the lay person's fast asks so little of the Christian that it is hard to imagine the fathers would find it efficacious as a real exercise in self-denial. In itself, our fast is simply not the same kind of tool as the fast of the desert.

What, then, is fasting, as it is performed by lay people, really for? The *Conferences* provide an answer. In the twenty-first conference, Abba Theonas discusses the reason that the Church first created the earliest fasting calendar by instituting the observance of Lent.

> It should be understood that the observance of Lent did not really exist so long as the perfection of the primitive Church

---

[19]   *Conf.* 5.XI.3.

remained intact. For they were not restricted by any obligation
to these principles ... since they fasted the whole length of the
year. Yet, when a large group of believers began declining day-
by-day from this apostolic devotion ... it seemed appropriate to
all the priests that those people who are tangled up in worldly
cares—and virtually ignorant (if I may say so) of abstinence and
repentance—should be reminded of the holy work of fasting by
having it imposed [on them].[20]

Abba Theonas, in fact, compares those worldly Christians for
whom Lent was created to Ananias and Sapphira who were struck
dead by the Holy Spirit for lying about their refusal to hand over
all their goods to the Church.[21] For him, Christians in the world
after the age of the apostles began to deny God their abstinence in
similar fashion. People like them began to take the Church from
a place where things like fasting happened all the time to a place
where they never happened at all.

In light of this problem, according to Abba Theonas, the
Church's fasting calendar was originally created as a means for
calling people in the world back to the pursuit of basic virtue,
which is to say back to the pursuit of purity of heart. While the
earliest Church, according to him, did not need such legalistic re-
straints to serve as a reminder of the essential Christian goal, the
laity of the later Church does. The requirements of Lent, he says,
do *not* actually emulate the strict ascesis of the early Church or the
desert. The really righteous person, he teaches, will fast well beyond
the demands of Lent.[22] As such, the fast of the Church calendar
is a kind of pantomime of desert abstinence—not genuinely very
ascetic in itself, but a nod to real thing.

Thus, the fasting of lay people, in accordance with the teachings of Abba Theonas, really has only a little to do with restraining
the will through the force of abstinence. Instead, fasting in accordance with the Church calendar infuses into Christian life a

---

[20]   *Conf.* 21.XXX.1–2.
[21]   Acts 5.1–6
[22]   *Conf.* 21.XXIX.2.

rhythm that calls the mind back to the pursuit of purity of heart. It makes our struggle against sin material, but not in the sense of serious bodily denial. Rather, it infuses materiality into our pursuit of purity of heart by affecting, according to a cycle, the things that we eat rather than introducing real hunger. It thus does much more to remind us of the material nature of our battle with sin than it does to really impact that battle on the physical plane. Facing that bowl of lentil soup that would have been a feast to Abba Moses, the mind ought to be drawn to remember that we must make real and actual the work of seeking purity of heart through our lives in society, our families, our work, and the rest. We deny ourselves almost nothing of food, but in denying just a little on fixed dates throughout the year, we remember that we must really go out and struggle to cultivate the virtue to which we know that we are called.

It is important that this not be misunderstood as a potential excuse to take Orthodox fasting lightly, or merely pay lip service to those fasting days that we are meant to observe. Abba Theonas' teaching implies just the opposite. For him, the fast of Lent (and by extension the other fasts on the calendar) is an absolute minimum in the spiritual life of a Christian. It exists precisely to provide us with a material backstop to our tendency toward vices of all sorts. The Church, Abba Theonas teaches, has asked the minimum of us so that we will not find ourselves in a position in which we are asked nothing at all. As a minimum, therefore, the fasting calendar must be observed as maximally as possible within the Christian life.[23] If, after all, the rhythm of the calendar is nearly all we have as laity to remind us of the material nature of our struggle, then to fail to observe even *this* would be to virtually walk away from the pursuit of purity of heart altogether.

When understood this way, fasting as a lay person ought to strike us as a fairly easy burden. It requires very little to give up meat and dairy for part of the year. This, in turn, ought to help

---

[23] All due exceptions for health and the economy of a confessor observed, of course.

guide us to a great deal of humility. The fathers, as we have noted, are often concerned that monks will fast immoderately and thus become prideful about their abstinence. Such spiritual pride ought to be completely impossible for lay people (which is not to say that it *is* impossible, of course). Drawing us ever away from such pride and toward a memory of our goal, the rhythm of the fast should become a drum-beat call in our lives, inviting us to the material pursuit of purity of heart and reminding us of what we are here for, like a companion whispering over and over throughout the year that we are called to God's kingdom.

Many are the sign-posts of the Christian life according to the *Conferences*. The three discussed here are perhaps the most important, but throughout this book we have been continually reminded that, through the exercise of discretion, virtually every waking moment can become its own sign-post as well. As we approach our goal bit by bit, and, in so approaching it, continually realize how far away it remains, the *Conferences* remind us to remain faithful in our use of such resources as the Eucharist, confession, and fasting as reminders of our pursuit of purity of heart, and thus of our *telos*, the kingdom. We now turn to a discussion of the teachings of the *Conferences* on those religious practices through which we are at times given a taste of this kingdom itself, namely, prayer and contemplation.

Beholding the Kingdom: Prayer and Contemplation

Nothing is more important in the life of a desert monk than prayer. And, while lay people do not have nearly the amount of time that a monk has to devote to it, prayer is equally the most essential spiritual practice of those living in the world. The fathers of the *Conferences* talk a lot about prayer and the subtleties of mastering it. Their insights are often profound, and certainly it is of great benefit for anyone to explore their wisdom on the topic directly. However, we will leave aside an in-depth discussion of the practicalities of prayer as presented in the *Conferences*. Instead, in this section we will seek to identify the purpose of prayer in the life of people in the world. As we will come to see, prayer has two key functions for us. First, like Eucharist, confession, and fasting, prayer returns our attention to our pursuit of purity of heart. Second, and more importantly, prayer can lead the mind to *theoria*, or contemplation, and thus can provide the Christian with a foretaste of the kingdom of God, the *telos* of Christian life.

To proceed we must naturally have a clear definition of prayer according to the fathers. In the ninth conference, Abba Isaac teaches that there are four primary types of Christian prayer. These are: 1) supplication, 2) prayer proper, 3) intercession, and 4) thanksgiving.[24] Each type is important, but they do not all have the same spiritual function, and some are more appropriate to certain occasions or certain people than others. We will return to this point in a moment. Before that, we will briefly define the four types of prayer.

Abba Isaac defines supplication as "a call for help or a petition regarding sins."[25] We give supplication when we ask God's mercy and forgiveness for our failings. Such prayer quite clearly has a central place in Orthodox life. It is fundamental to all the services of the Church, and is foundational to both the Lord's prayer and the modern Jesus Prayer. Abba Isaac teaches that supplication is the most important kind of prayer for beginners who are still struggling to tame the vices.[26] The implication of his teaching is that supplicatory prayer functions much like discretion. To supplicate God for forgiveness of sins is to behold the ways in which we have deviated from our pursuit of purity of heart, and to implore God's aid in the work of turning back to that essential Christian goal.

According to Abba Isaac, the second kind of prayer—prayer proper—takes place "when we are laying bare or promising something to God."[27] He goes on to clarify what this means somewhat.

---

[24]   *Conf.* 9.IX.2.
[25]   Conf. 9.XI.
[26]   *Conf.* 9.XV.I.
[27]   *Conf.* 9.XII.I.

> We pray when, renouncing this world, we vow that we will serve
> the Lord with the total focus of our hearts, dead to all earthly
> affairs and activities. We pray when we promise to hold on to the
> Lord in our meekness of spirit and our absolute contrition of
> heart, disregarding worldly honor and rejecting earthly power.[28]

Prayer proper, then, is an outpouring of the human soul in reaction
to the realization of one's worldliness and sinfulness. It arises from
supplication as the natural extension of a pious heart that seeks
God's aid in overcoming sin. As we strive toward purity of heart,
growing ever more conscious of how far we are from this goal, we
naturally express to God our earnest desire not to turn back to
worldly things, but rather to keep our faith in the kingdom alone.
Our promises in this regard are frequently broken, yet we continue
to pledge them, and with each new pledge we mark our conscious
return to the pursuit of purity of heart.

Abba Isaac says that prayer proper is the most important type
for those who have already made good progress toward virtue.[29] It
is a step up from supplication because the act of pledging oneself
to God implies that one has not just realized one's own sin, but has
truly come to see its distastefulness and to desire its eradication.
If our supplications act as sign-posts back to purity of heart, our
prayers, properly defined, constitute our consent to pursue this
goal once again.

The third form of prayer, according to Abba Isaac, is intercession. This is prayer that we make "for somebody else … begging
for peace for our loved-ones, of course, and also for the whole
world."[30] In essence, intercessory prayer is prayer that overflows
from us when we have touched something of real purity of heart.
In those moments when we find ourselves at peace (relatively
speaking) about our own sins and commitment to the pursuit of
our Christian goal, our hearts naturally turn to those around us,

---

[28]   *Conf.* 9.XII.2.
[29]   *Conf.* 9.XV.1.
[30]   *Conf.* 9.XIII.

desiring the same peace for them, and the same pursuit of purity of heart.

Abba Isaac teaches that intercessory prayer is especially for "those who accomplish perfection in their vows ... and are called to intercede for others out of concern for their weakness and the fondness of love."[31] The implication is that those still struggling with their own sins are not really in a position to intercede for others. This ought not to be taken too rigidly, as Abba Isaac himself will note below, but the fact that he presents prayers of intercession mainly as the domain of the more spiritually elevated than supplications and prayer proper does have important implications for its role in lay life. For us, to realize that we desire God's aid for another person should be, simultaneously, to realize that we desire God's aid for us as well. Conversely, if we see another person struggling in life, we should see also our own struggles and shortcomings. The friend, family member, neighbor, or stranger for whom we pray should serve as a mirror into ourselves as we realize that we act as one sinner praying for another. Thus, to pray for another person, at least for us lay people, invites us to return to our own pursuit as much as it beseeches God's aid for that person. It is, yet again, a sign-post on the way.

The fourth and highest kind of prayer, according to Abba Isaac, is thanksgiving. In moments of such prayer, we think about all God's blessing in the past, present and future such that the mind "answers back to the Lord by way of indescribable ecstasies."[32] In thanksgiving we reflect not on our own brokenness or on the distance we find ourselves from our *telos* and goal, but rather on the goodness of the *telos* and goal themselves. From prayers growing out of our suffering in the face of our own brokenness, we elevate the mind to prayers that pour forward joy at the thought of the good gifts that we receive and will receive from God. We thus find ourselves desiring purity of heart and the kingdom of God not

[31]   *Conf.* 9.XV.1.
[32]   *Conf.* 9.XIV.

out of a sense of obligation, conscience, or fear, but rather out of genuine love for these things—driven *to* them as ultimate goods rather than being driven from sin as an evil. For this reason, Abba Isaac teaches that this kind of prayer is especially for those who have conquered the vices, and can now focus their minds solely on the mercy of God.[33]

It is already clear that, according to Abba Isaac, there is a hierarchy within these forms of prayer. While all are important for all people, they are nonetheless each in turn more desirable and more perfect than the previous form.

> Still, as we make headway in life and attain to virtue, we should firmly seek, if possible, those kinds of prayer that pour out from the contemplation of good things to come [thanksgiving], or from the warmth of love [intercession].[34]

Abba Isaac's understanding of this hierarchy does not, it would seem, grow out of a sense that supplicatory prayer or prayer proper are, in themselves, inferior to intercession and thanksgiving. Indeed, supplication and prayer are exactly what is required for those who most need God's aid in returning to their pursuit of purity of heart. Instead, the superior status that he ascribes to intercession and thanksgiving grows from his desire that every Christian come to the point in their pursuit of purity of heart at which prayers of intercession and thanksgiving become our primary ways of praying. He wants us to see the beautiful Good that is our goal and desire it in joy for ourselves and all those around us, no longer stumbling on our way. To seek purity of heart and the kingdom for such reasons is without question the most beautiful human impulse conceivable.

We can thus make our first key observation about the nature of prayer in the lay life. Prayer is both the last, and most critical, of the key sign-posts directing us to purity of heart. And, indeed, it is our steadfast companion when we actually begin to really approach this goal, at least now and then. When we see that we have fallen

---

[33] *Conf.* 9.XV.I.
[34] *Conf.* 9.XVI.

from our pursuit, it is most especially through intercession that
we seek God's aid in returning. When we commit to our goal once
again, it is especially through prayer proper that we declare this
commitment. When we see the goodness of this goal for others,
it is through intercession that we pour out our desire for them to
taste the goal, and again renew that same desire within ourselves.
And when we begin now and then really to see the beauty of the
telos to which purity of heart leads us, our souls leap forward with
thanksgiving. As such, prayer, unlike virtually any other spiritual
tool in the Christian life, is of benefit to the Christian in absolutely
any situation or any spiritual state. We may not always be well advised to approach the Eucharist, receive confession, or fast. But,
because our way of praying adapts itself to our spiritual situation,
our frame of mind, our mood, and any other condition in which
we find ourselves, prayer is always with us.

> Everyone prays differently when he is upbeat from when he is
> weighed down by the burden of sadness or despair, and differ-
> ently when he is buoyed by spiritual success from when he is sunk
> by a glut of attacks, and differently when he pleads for forgiveness
> of sins, or when he asks to acquire grace, or begs for the elimina-
> tion of a particular vice.[35]

Prayer molds itself to our condition, and so is the perennial tool
of the Christian, whether it serves as a reminder to seek purity
of heart, or a thanksgiving for the same purity when it is briefly
experienced.

For Abba Isaac, then, the four forms of prayer spill into one
another in a chain, and this spilling forward is reflective of the
Christian growth in purity of heart. Yet, even prayers of thanksgiving are not the highest and most sublime of human experiences.
There remains one final prayerful state, which he does not explicitly name, that rises above all others.

> Sometimes, though, a mind that makes progress toward that true
> state of purity (and that begins to take root in such a state) starts

---

[35]   *Conf.* 9.VIII.3.

to draw in all these [kinds of prayer] at once, and like some incomprehensible and furious flame, it flies through all of them, and pours out prayers that cannot be described—utterly pure and fervent—prayers that the Spirit itself gives to God, bursting in with groans indescribable, unknown to us [Cf. Rom 8.26], and in that moment of supplication, grasping and pouring out things so ungraspable that not only can they not pass over the lips, but, I tell you, they cannot even be remembered by the mind later on.[36]

Here, Abba Isaac is describing a state of consciousness that we discussed in chapter one—he is describing *theoria*, which can be translated as "contemplation."

As we said in chapter one, contemplation is, for the fathers of the *Conferences,* the most important effect of Christian virtue and the most desirable state of the human mind. In true contemplation, the mind draws as close to God as possible in this life in an experience (later often described as the experience of the divine light) that cannot possibly be captured in words. Contemplation is a foretaste of the kingdom of God—the real presence of our ultimate *telos* made manifest to the Christian in the present moment.

The most essential purpose of prayer according to Abba Isaac, then, is to lead the mind toward this kind of *theoria*. As much as prayer functions to help direct us continually to our pursuit of purity of heart, it also has a profound capacity to lead the mind beyond this pursuit and connect the Christian directly, if momentarily, with the actual *telos* of our lives. Prayer, for the fathers, is like a sign along the road that contains within itself not just good directions, but also a perfect image of the destination—a manifestation of what it is we are seeking in the end. To experience moments of *theoria*, then, is to experience our *telos* partially and temporarily. Through grace, God gives us such moments as a promise and a reminder—to assure us that we are not merely left to dream fantastical things about what is in store for us in the kingdom, but are invited to really experience some of what we are

---

[36] *Conf.* 9.XV.2.

seeking, to know the nature of the kingdom as one who has been there, even while its fullness still awaits us in the future.

As such, according to the fathers, when we taste the fullness of contemplation, we realize that all other good things in life pale in comparison to it. So lofty is the experience of *theoria* that the many virtues and good works that we strive so much to cultivate in our lives—those things that lead to purity of heart—all seem almost worthless. Abba Theonas teaches this in the twenty-third conference

> So, while the value of each of the virtues that I have delineated above is great (the virtues are good things in themselves), still they look dark by comparison to the brightness of *theoria*. For being focused on earthly concerns (even good works) greatly interferes with and distracts holy people from the contemplation of the highest good.... So, the blessed David wishes for [*theoria*] alone in defining the act of clinging to God as that which is good for human beings, saying, "it is good for me to cling to God, and to put my hope in the Lord" [Ps 73.28].[37]

The human being in contemplation is like King David, hoping in the Lord. In the same vein, the conferences teach that the Christian in contemplation experiences something of what St Peter did when beholding the transfiguration of Jesus. In the Gospel account Peter says, "Lord, it is good for us to be here," and pours out his desire to remain forever on the mountain in the sight of the uncreated light, never returning again to the world, and the ministry that is his duty there.[38] Yet, as Abba Theonas teaches (and the story of the transfiguration reflects) human beings cannot stay in a state of contemplation forever. Even the most devoted of all monks must cease his prayers of *theoria* from time to time and tend to the necessities of life. They are, in this regard, much like the Apostle Paul who was repeatedly forced away from contemplation to tend to the needs of life.[39]

[37] *Conf.* 23.IV.4–V.2.
[38] Mt 17.4.
[39] *Conf.* 23.V.4.

Still, according to the fathers of the *Conferences*, great progress can be made toward more continual *theoria* through the practice of ceaseless prayer, a practice we have already discussed in relation to its application in regards to work. The pursuit of constant prayer has its roots in scripture; the desert monks took quite literally the injunction of the Apostle Paul that we should "pray without ceasing."[40] In order to cultivate such ceaseless prayer, Abba Isaac (like many other monastic authors) recommends that Christians get in the habit of repeating a simple prayer as often as possible until they find themselves repeating it absolutely constantly. We noted in the previous chapter the formula that Abba Isaac prefers: "oh God, make speed to save me, oh Lord, make haste to help me, "[41] a predecessor of the modern Jesus Prayer. Abba Isaac recommends that monks focus their attention on this prayer whenever they can, clearing their minds of all other thoughts. By repeating it, the Christian can grow in their experience of *theoria*.

> Steeping the heart in this [brief prayer above] (which becomes a saving habit for you) will protect you not just from every assault of the demons, but will also lead you to *theoria* directed toward invisible and heavenly things, clearing out every earthly vice and impurity from you; and it will carry you to the indescribable warmth of the prayer that so few people experience.[42]

Abba Isaac recommends literally repeating the same simple prayer all the time without stopping, first thing in the morning, through the day including times of work, and even just before bed so that one actually learns to pray in his sleep.[43] When prayer never stops, *theoria* can be touched more often and for longer periods of time.

For a person in the world, absolutely ceaseless verbal prayer, even of the simplest words, is not likely possible. Yet, there is a certain pessimistic implication of Abba Isaac's teaching about repetitive

---

[40]   I Thess 5.17.
[41]   *Conf.* 10.X.2.
[42]   *Conf.* 10.X.14.
[43]   *Conf.* 10.X.15.

prayers that sheds light on how the laity ought to approach this problem. Abba Isaac assumes that ceaseless prayer will take a long time for a monk to master. To pray ceaselessly is not something a person merely begins to do over night. Instead, it is, for Abba Isaac, a project like that of children learning to write the alphabet, who have to draw their letters over and over again until they can do so with ease.[44] Simple repetitive prayer is, quite literally, an exercise, designed to help the mind turn its focus more and more to *theoria* over time. The implication of this for us is simple. Repetitive prayer will be spiritually beneficial when done to any degree. It is not an all or nothing practice. As such, to introduce some repetitive prayer into lay life will have a profound effect on us.

There is an essential question that has been hanging over our discussion so far. Can lay people ever really experience *theoria* at all, or is it the business of monks alone? The *Conferences* do not give an explicit answer, but in light of what we have said about *theoria* and continual prayer to this point, it is my firm conviction that the answer is yes. While *theoria* will never be a major part of a life in the world, it can, at times, be a small part if the teachings of the fathers on prayer are carried out as much as possible.

To do this, the lay person must begin by simply praying when she can. While a professional athlete certainly works out a great deal more than the average school teacher, it remains the case that what exercise is possible for that teacher will be of benefit to her health. So it is with the life of prayer. The lay Christian must sow the seeds of prayer as often as possible, and hope (indeed, pray) that some of them will grow. If ceaseless prayer is the ideal of the monk, then frequent prayer is the least that we as lay people can expect from ourselves. In frequently praying, we must strive to make *theoria* a part of our lives despite the fact that it will never be as big a part as it is in the lives of the desert monks. For, knowing that in contemplation we are invited by God to taste his kingdom, it would be madness to make no effort at all to accept this invitation.

[44]   *Conf.* 10.X.1.

Still, in a lay life of frequent prayer, moments of real *theoria* will remain sparse, or may never actually come about despite our pious seeking of them. To begin with, most of our prayer life will center primarily on supplication and prayer proper, and so even most of the hours we devote to prayer will not lead us to *theoria*, nor should we expect them to. What is more, if St Paul and the monks of the desert were forced away from their contemplation to earn their living, we are forced away from this state far more often for the same reason. If they hoped to pray so constantly that they even continued their prayers in their sleep, we hope to stick to a rule that demands of us prayer a few times a day. As such, the opportunities for our prayers to spill out into *theoria* are few.

At first blush, this fact may invite some despair. How great is the gift of *theoria* and yet how little will we touch it! What hope is there for a person who is so rarely, or perhaps never at all, able to elevate his mind to that state that the desert monks held above all others? Yet, when we consider our situation soberly we ought to see things the other way around. We ought to realize how tremendous a gift we receive if our minds are elevated even once in a lifetime to real *theoria*. For *theoria* is a taste of the kingdom that we anticipate with hope, and it is accompanied by the promise that this kingdom will be made fully manifest in God's time. As the fathers teach, no one in this life remains in a state of true contemplation forever. Its purpose for us in the present is not to become permanent. Rather, it is to act as a beacon and reminder of our Christian *telos*. What despair can we maintain in light of even the tiniest moment in the light of such a beacon? For it is not the frequency or length of such experiences that makes them important in Christian life—it is the assurance that they hold of the nature of the kingdom. Short and rare as *theoria* will ever be, if it happens at all for us, its presence to any degree is already the fullness of the blessing that it gives.

Thus, the patient, prayerful, life-long quest to experience *theoria* ought to provide us with a profound sense of hope as lay people. Our lives in the world are so often a mad spiritual chaos—a sine wave of ups and downs—a desperate seeking of something beyond, but something that never seems to become wholly manifest. We repent of our sins, and commit the same ones again and again. We love as true Christian friends for a moment, only to find ourselves furious with anger a little while later. We give selflessly, then suddenly feel pangs of greed. We pray for a while, and then are distracted by endless worldly thoughts. Yet, what we see and realize in those moments in which we experience the kingdom in contemplation, and what we, in fact, intuitively understand just by looking for these moments, is that God has promised us that this, the endless struggle of our lives in the world, is fleeting and relative. In seeking *theoria* we understand that what is promised to us as our real *telos* is not a life in which we simply do better in our pursuit of purity of heart. The life of the kingdom is not merely an improved existence of essentially the same nature as this one, as if a time in which we become less sinful sinners, or patched-up but still broken people. No, we in the world await our real *telos* in which holiness, love, and light are the *essence* of human existence—the totality of what we are—not something grafted on to us, but the core reality of the human self. We await our future re-creation in which we are so filled with the presence of God that we merge and become one with him. We long for an existence so profoundly transformed that we can scarcely recognize it in comparison to our lives as they are at present. We behold, or at least seek, fleeting visions of such an existence in *theoria*.

We must make a final observation here about *theoria* as it relates to worldly life in particular, as opposed to life in the desert. We as people in the world should react to what we do manage to experience in *theoria* not primarily with efforts to come into contemplation more and more constantly (the kinds of efforts the desert fathers made), but rather with a renewed and hopeful commitment to the lives in the world to which we have been called, and especially to those places within these lives in which the kingdom of God can become manifest in much the same way that it does in contemplation—places like the love of true friendship, unity of purpose in a family, or married sexuality. In short, in our rare glimpses of the kingdom, the whole world and everything in it should start to become a reminder of our *telos*.

> But the contemplation of God is gained in a variety of ways. For we not only discover God by admiring his incomprehensible essence (a thing that still lies hidden in the hope of his promise), but we see him through the greatness of his creation, and the consideration of his justice, and the aid of his daily providence: when with pure minds we contemplate what he has done with his saints in every generation, when with trembling hearts we admire the power with which he governs, directs and rules all things, or the vastness of his knowledge, or that eye of his from which no secrets of the heart can lie hidden—when we consider the sand of the sea, and the number of the waves measured by him and known to him, when in our wonder we think that the drops of rain, the days and hours of the ages, and all things past and future are present to his knowledge; when we gaze in unbounded admiration on that ineffable mercy of his, which endures with unwearied patience countless sins (every moment being committed under his very eyes) ... for he himself, overcoming the enemy in us simply for the pleasure of his good will, rewards us with eternal bliss and everlasting rewards, for in these days he undertook the dispensation of his incarnation for our salvation.[45]

So teaches Abba Moses in the first conference, and so do we come full circle in our discussion throughout this book. For here we see that in light of what is revealed in Christian *theoria*, the chiefest, but by no means exclusive, foretaste of the kingdom, every aspect of the creation, from our own participation in that creation in marriage, to every experience at work, to every falling down and return to the path of purity of heart, to every moment of joy and every moment of anguish, to every relationship we have with every human being we encounter, to our freedom from the slavery of material things, to every gift of charity, to every moment of reflection in discretion, to every confession, to every fast, to every prayer, to all things that we behold in every direction, within and

---

[45] *Conf.* I.XV.1–2. Translation adapted from Gibson.

without—all of them direct the mind to the magnificence of the kingdom of God alone.

The value of prayerful *theoria* is in giving us a picture of what we are looking for. We do not seek to spend less and less time in the world, and more and more time in contemplative prayer. We seek instead to use prayer to open up our own eyes so that the lives that we really live are lives in which it becomes impossible to lose sight of the kingdom at every moment—impossible to forget because it is so manifest in everything around us.

Concluding Remarks

The great spiritual practices that make Orthodox life unique are essential to the life of people in the world. Yet, they are not the *essence* of this life—they are, instead, the most important ways that we remind ourselves of what we are seeking as our end and goal. We seek purity of heart and the kingdom in and through the world, and lean upon the Eucharist, confession, fasting, and prayer as means to focus our minds on what it is we have set out to do.

To mistake these spiritual practices as our essential way of being Christian, or to abandon them in neglect, are both errors that create a division in our lives that places us in a hopeless situation as Christians. If our daily grind amounts to nothing more than a distraction from prayer, then we make of ourselves not holy people, but simply profoundly lazy monks who have taken on so many worldly distractions that they cannot possibly make progress in their real work. To refuse to engage these practices at all, conversely, makes it impossible for us to see what human life is for, and thus makes it impossible for us to pursue our end and goal in the world or anywhere else. To be a lay person in the first mold is to be like a man who chooses to eat nothing but junk food despite having a cupboard full of nutritious fare. To be a lay person in the second mold is to be one who fails even to open that same cupboard in the first place. Such fools should probably not expect much in the way of health.

But the fathers of the *Conferences* do not encourage either mistake with regard to religious practices. Instead, they see these practices as beacons that call us back to purity of heart, and that grant us a taste of the kingdom. Understood in accordance with their teachings, then, the Eucharist, confession, fasting and prayer become essential tools in the life of lay Christians as they struggle in and through the world to cultivate purity of heart and reach the kingdom of God.

Conclusion

The problem of lay life is one about which many in the Christian world, whether Orthodox or otherwise, frequently struggle today. In a Western culture that deeply values equality and participation for all people in all aspects of political and social life, we frequently struggle to articulate the place of lay people in the Church. Quite often, especially outside Orthodoxy, it is assumed that the Church ought to more fully resemble the civic life of the world. Many rail against clericalism or monasticism as creating a hierarchy that denigrates lay people to the status of second-class religious citizens. Many more seek to diminish the role of asceticism, prayer, or confession in religious life on the grounds that these things make Christianity hard, and thus exclude the masses too much. Still others battle against ancient practices like closed communion or the male-only priesthood because they create barriers to universal participation in religious life.

This problem of participation in Christian life is without question real and pressing, but I do not wish to comment directly here on any of the particular issues just brought up as examples of its symptoms. Instead, I mention such problems simply to note that I worry very much about certain of the assumptions that seem to be made by many Christians when offering solutions to them. It seems to me that a key operating principles behind many of the most popular responses to the problem of the laity today is that the best way to make lay life meaningful is to encourage lay people to become more deeply involved in the leadership and religious life of the Church.

Perhaps in some respects this is a good idea, and, as I said, I am not interested in weighing in on any specifics now. Yet, I am left with a great sense of worry that in seeking to enlist more and more lay people in those aspects of Church life that were once the business of specialists like monks, nuns, and priests, we may cheapen the real Christian work of the laity to the point that we lose sight of it altogether. It may feel welcoming and inclusive to encourage lay people to strive to become leaders in their communities in every possible way, in some cases outside of Orthodoxy to the point of eliminating the priesthood along with monasticism altogether. Yet, if we do this at the expense of the recognition that lay life itself, exactly as it already is, is a holy and divine calling, then I fear we do far more harm than good in the end. My concern, in sum, is that we have spent too long as Christians actually agreeing to the notion that lay life is second-rate and only marginally spiritual. Perhaps it is actually our agreement with such a false approach to the laity that fuels many of our attempts at greater "inclusiveness."

Again, discussing politics is not the point of this book. I bring these issues up for just a moment because thinking about them is one of the best ways for us to focus our picture of what it is that we *have* been trying to establish by reading the fathers of the *Conferences* in light of lay life. In place of wringing our hands about how to change the experience of lay Christians, include them more as leaders, or find new explicitly religious meaning to infuse into their lives, we have been seeking in this book to use monastic literature to draw out what meaning is already present in lay life right now, exactly as it is. Our hope has been to rediscover the light yoke of Christ, which is already right in front of our faces and requires no efforts of politicking or revolution to reclaim. I hope in some small way that this work has made it a little more easy to see that lay life in the Orthodox Church is life defined by a profoundly challenging and holy call—the same holy call of all Christian life—in our case, lived out in the particular context that life in the world happens to present. A life lived for such a call is a life of struggle for purity of heart and the kingdom of God, which struggle we take on here in the cities and towns of the world, surrounded by every imaginable impediment to holiness. In my view, the greatest problem presented by the laity today is that we have forgotten what a tremendous series of spiritual responsibilities and opportunities are already presented to us simply by waking up in the morning and walking out the door.

As such, my hope is that lay readers of this book will see their Christian lives in our world *not* as more easily managed than before they began reading, but as far more challenging. To put it simply, Christian life makes immense demands on the human being. Ours is not a faith attended to once a week or a few times a year. Christ accepts nothing less than the whole of our existence. He demands nothing short of our every waking moment. He leads us to nothing other than his kingdom realized in the absolute holiness of purity of heart. Lay life must reflect all of these things. Our way of living it must bear witness to our recognition that a total life in Christ is not the business of a handful of monks and nuns, along with a few of the better priests—but that it is a life meant for all human beings, and one meant to begin *now* and *here*, in our lives as they are on this very day, not after our death or some time in the future, nor in those few moments when we can escape our world a little, nor only in those quiet corners of a chapel or prayer room.

Yet, in the same stroke, I hope that this book offers great comfort to the reader. Indeed, to take seriously our lives as lay Christians is to see them as profoundly demanding, but it is also to see them as lives wherein the kingdom of God is potentially manifest everywhere. Just as Christ demands no less of us than he does of the fathers of the desert, even while demanding something different, so he also offers us no fewer signs of his kingdom than they.

To realize one's call to life in the world is not to accept that one is too weak to be a monk. Instead, it is to realize that the particular signs of the kingdom offered specifically to worldly people are the signs for which we as individuals were created to live. This is a realization that we must experience in the very depths of our soul. As the fathers of the desert sought asceticism and contemplation with all the love and vigor that they could muster, knowing that through these things they touched their real *telos* in the kingdom, so we must seek with all our strength the *telos* of the kingdom manifest in our homes, in our parishes, in our work, and above all in the fullness of the love we experience for the people around us—strangers, friends, children, and spouses. To know that we are lay people is to know that it is these particular things, when they become what we know they can really be, that ring the bell of our soul.

Abba Theonas speaks of people in the world this way.

> Thus, they realize that it is not possible to attain their desired *telos* by human strength (thanks to the stubborn burden of the flesh), nor is it possible to be united with the greatest and highest good (though this is their heart's desire), but that they are dragged like hostages away from the sight of it and toward worldly things. And so, they gravitate toward the grace of God "who justifies the impious" [Rom 4.5], and they cry out with the apostle, "I am a wretched man: what will liberate me from this body of death? The grace of God through our Lord, Jesus Christ" [Rom 7.24–25].[1]

This hard burden of life in the world, impossible as it really is to live in the holiness to which we know it could bring us, gives perhaps its greatest blessing of all in reminding us of the need to turn to God alone for our salvation. For it is never through our efforts, in the end, that we come to purity of heart. It was, after all, purity of heart for which we were originally created, and thus to be holy is simply to be human—it is no accomplishment, and no feat. To taste the kingdom, to really live there, is to be with God himself—a gift from something utterly beyond us and beyond even the whole of the creation. We, broken by the world, see this more clearly than anyone. But we remember, too, that this God does not meet only his holy monks and nuns, nor only his priests and bishops, to bear them up from their impossible state into his kingdom. He meets also us, we laymen lost in the desert that the city has become.

---

[1]   *Conf* 23.X.1.

I hope by the same grace of God that we have merely scratched the surface here of a far deeper conversation about the life of lay Orthodox Christians and its potential saving power. For now, let this small essay suffice, and so let me conclude by recording St John's final words in the *Conferences* as if they were my own. "All that remains is for me—a man sent off course by a most dangerous tempest—to be brought to the safe harbor of silence by the wind of your breath in your prayers."[2]

---

[2]   *Conf.* 24.XXVI.19.

Some Further Reading on St John Cassian

Casiday, Augustine. *Tradition and Theology in St John Cassian*. Oxford: Oxford, 2007.

Driver, Steven D. *John Cassian and the Reading of Egyptian Monastic Culture*. London: Routledge, 2002.

Funk, Mary Margaret. *Thoughts Matter: The Practice of the Spiritual Life*. London: Continuum, 1998.

Goodrich, Richard J. *Contextualizing Cassian: Aristocrats, Asceticism, and Reformation in Fifth-Century Gaul*. Oxford: Oxford, 2007.

Merton, Thomas. *Cassian and the Fathers: Initiation into the Monastic Tradition*. Collegeville: Cistercian, 2004.

Ramsey, Boniface. *John Cassian: The Conferences*. New York: Newman, 1997.

Rousseau, Philip. *Ascetics, Authority and the Church in the Age of Jerome and Cassian*. Oxford: Oxford, 1978.

Stewart, Columba. *Cassian the Monk*. Oxford: Oxford, 1998.